Whose Witnesses?

"Whosoever transgresses, and does not abide in the doctrine of Christ, does not have God…"
"If anyone comes to you and does not bring this doctrine, do not receive him into your house…"

2 John 9 & 10

By Cheryl Arnold

Copyright © 2009 by Cheryl Arnold

Whose Witnesses?
"Whosoever transgresses, and does not abide in the doctrine of Christ, does not have God..."
"If anyone comes to you and does not bring this doctrine, do not receive him into your house..." 2 John 9 & 10
by Cheryl Arnold

Printed in the United States of America

ISBN 9781615796786

All rights reserved solely by the author. The author guarantees all contents are original and do not infringe upon the legal rights of any other person or work. No part of this book may be reproduced in any form without the permission of the author. The views expressed in this book are not necessarily those of the publisher.

Unless otherwise indicated, Bible quotations are taken from The Holy Bible, Authorized King James Version of the Bible. Copyright © 1999 by Holman Bible Publishers.

www.xulonpress.com

Table of Contents

Chapter One	Knock, Knock, Who's There?	9
Chapter Two	Whose Witnesses?	13
Chapter Three	Identifying the Counterfeit	17
Chapter Four	What the Witnesses Believe	20
Chapter Five	Who Does Jesus Say He is?	23

Dedication

I would like to dedicate this book to my precious family: To my wonderful husband, Tim, who is the love of my life and my best friend; also to my two beautiful children, Garrett and Melanie. God has blessed me with the most wonderful family I could ever ask for and they fill my life with joy and laughter.

And most of all I would like to dedicate this book to my Lord, Jesus Christ, who has graciously redeemed me from the pit, has dressed me in garments of white and has sealed me with His Spirit for all eternity and now calls me His beloved. I am so amazed that He has trusted me with His Word.

Chapter One

Knock, Knock, Who's There?

I awoke this morning and began a wonderful time with God in prayer and in the study of His Word. I had the morning to myself and the leisure to sit comfortably before Him and just listen. He speaks so readily to us if we desire to hear from Him.

I guess it was around 10:30 when I heard the doorbell ring. I had been lingering a little longer than was normal and really needed to be getting a shower so I could begin my day of work, which consists of retreating to my sewing room in the back of my house where my husband Tim has built me a cozy little sewing shop. I make slipcovers for a living.

I was right there in the living room in my robe with my hair a mess, sporting my usual disheveled morning look, when without warning the visitors came. I had no choice but to go to the door and present myself as I was…and it was not pretty, I'll tell you that. Anyway, I opened the door and two young ladies were standing there. Though they looked innocent enough, I immediately suspected that they were Jehovah's Witnesses but realized that I must be mistaken when they asked me something unexpected.

One of the ladies said, "Hello, we are in the neighborhood and just wanted to know if you knew of anyone who is deaf and may need some assistance." I was confused. I thought for a moment and realized that I really didn't know of anyone who is deaf.

Well, after pondering that for a moment, my mind came back to the present and I said to them, "So you aren't Jehovah's Witnesses then?"

And I don't know whether or not I was surprised when their answer came. "Yes, we are" they said.

"Hmmm"....I thought. "That is very sneaky." "The Witnesses are sharpening their deception skills, and by golly, they almost got me...almost."

After pausing for a moment to assess their true motives I said to them, "That is very deceitful." "You're not really here to ask if you can assist anyone who is deaf." Then I said to them, because it was the honest and most immediate thought that came to me: "God is never deceitful." Then I said, "Satan is deceitful, but God is not."

Now I could be wrong but I suspect that they justified their misleading behavior by telling themselves that by "deaf" they meant those whose ears have not been opened to the truth of God...just a hunch. But still, their motives were definitely clandestine. Their intent was to deceive.

After that I began to let flow what God had in that instant placed on my heart to speak to these deceived young ladies. They thought they were on a holy mission from God but were in truth just the latest victims of Satan's ageless efforts to thwart God's perfect plan by deceiving as many as he can.

I told them about another young man who had come by a few months ago (also a Jehovah's Witness in disguise) with the same sort of story. He was masking who he really was in order to trick and deceive. I told them that John tells us, and warns us even, in 2 John, that the one who comes to our door bringing a different gospel than the gospel of Christ (which is what the Jehovah's Witnesses do) has the spirit of antichrist and should not be even invited into our house, lest we partake of their evil.

I also warned these two women who had been deceived, that they belonged to a cult that denied the true gospel and that the only way to God was through the saving blood of Jesus Christ. That was the end of our conversation. They turned about very kindly and left, not wanting to press their point any longer. The Word tells us to "Resist the devil and he will flee" (James 4:7).

I am thinking of a perfect analogy that describes so well what they are doing. I don't want to be rude but this really fits, even though it is very funny. Here it is: There are exterminator commercials running right now that make me laugh when I see them. The doorbell rings at some house and when the homeowner opens the door, there is a giant termite wanting to get in. He pretends to be someone else but has his eyes on the delectable wood flooring that he plans to devour once he gains access to it. He just wants to get in…he'll say anything to get in. I don't want to be overly aggressive here with Witnesses but what they are peddling is not at all innocent so I will call things as I see them. They are after all going door to door trampling the name of God underfoot and I believe that deserves an appropriate response. My heart is to speak the truth.

In the same way that the intruder is depicted in the commercial, Satan has deceived many who have followed this false gospel of the Jehovah's Witnesses and has sent them out to "just get in the door" of any vulnerable and unsuspecting victim. He also wants to devour (1 Peter 5:8).

My desire is that God's people will rise up today and expose this false religion for what it truly is. Now I know that the Jehovah's Witnesses are only one of so many more false religions out there but I am moved to expose this particular one because it is very close to my heart. You see, my mother was a Jehovah's Witness and I believe she probably died without

Christ. There is always hope that she had met with Him at some point before her death but if she did I have no knowledge of that. I was beside her when she took her last breath.

I did not become a believer until sometime after my mother's death, but curiously I remember always asking her why she never liked talking about Jesus. She seemed to always avoid talking about Him and even though I was not a Christian then, somehow I knew that it was wrong of her to do that. It felt wrong. It was wrong. But what else could she have done? She followed a religion that does not honor Jesus as God, so she didn't either.

God had mercy on me and led me to Him in spite of my growing up without Him. It makes me very sad that my mother never desired Christ or anything He offered. She had been a victim of the lies and deceit herself, having parents who were deeply caught-up in this organization. She had been duped into thinking that her good works would get her into heaven; that if she were good enough and followed the Witnesses closely enough, and knocked on enough doors that she could maybe, just maybe, be one of the special 144,000 who will be allowed to enter heaven.

Oh my heart is heavy for those who are caught up in these lies. It's heavier still for those who have yet to be tainted by these lies, but soon will be. It's just a matter of that doorbell ringing and an uninformed and lonely heart on the other side of that door inviting deception and death into their living room, and the damage is done.

I know there are so many wonderful books out there that expose this particular cult and explain very clearly with the Word of God how far from the truth their doctrine really is and I am so thankful. But God has recently put it on my heart to write what little I know about the lies that the Jehovah's Witnesses teach and how the truth of the Bible clearly exposes them for who they are and who it really is they are witnesses for.

Chapter Two

Whose Witnesses?

The title of this chapter and of this book, "Whose Witnesses?" is truly not intended to relate any sort of sarcasm. But it is honest. Who are these people witnessing for? Who has sent them? They say and believe that it is Jehovah God but I will show how it is not Jehovah God who has sent them. I think it is an important question to ask and I ask it with all sincerity. It is not Jehovah God who has sent them, and that's what I intend to prove. I think I can reveal with even my limited knowledge of who they are, that they are not witnessing for the one true God, Jehovah; the God of the Bible. They may think they are, but their god is an impostor. He is one who the Bible says disguises himself as an angel of light. What a pattern here…look at how at these last two visits, the Jehovah's Witnesses used disguise and deception. It is very telling. Jesus said Satan is a liar and the father of lies. He said there is no truth in Satan and there never was.

The prophet Isaiah told us in Isaiah 14 that Satan desired to be God. Ezekiel tells us in Ezekiel 28 that Satan is destined for damnation and his future has already been determined. He began his wicked plan in the Garden of Eden when he deceived Eve and has continued throughout all of history to deceive nation after nation, and people after people. He knows his future but this has not stopped him from trying to bring down with him as many of God's creation as he can. His favorite weapon is deception and he is a master at it.

He has been behind the attempted annihilation of the Jews throughout all of history. He is behind every false religion in the world. He is behind all that is in opposition to the one true God. He has attempted to confuse, distort and deny the Word of God. He has infiltrated some of the church. He has torn apart families and has wreaked havoc on the earth.

His particular hatred is for God. He wants God's throne and desires to receive His worship. The focus of his diabolical plan is on the Son of God. He knows that if he can keep the truth of the gospel away from men then they are doomed...he knows that. He knows the truth but despises it because it condemns him. There is no hope for Satan. His time is limited and the victory is Christ's therefore he hates our God and His Christ.

Satan has a calling card. It is easily identifiable if we belong to God but craftily hidden if we do not. He denies that Jesus is God in the flesh...even though he knows this is the truth; both he and his demons know it and tremble. I'll say it again and give the statement its own line because in this book, this is the claim of the Witnesses that I will prove false using the Word of God. The Jehovah's Witnesses want you to believe one thing:

They claim and spend all of their time trying to convince others that Jesus Christ is not God.

Satan knows that Jesus is God. He just doesn't want anyone else to know that because if we don't believe that Jesus is God and that He died on the cross for our sin then we cannot be saved and enter Heaven. He knows the truth therefore it is this truth that he always attacks. All false religions and all cults go for the jugular. They deny that Christ is God in the flesh and deny that His blood is the only atoning sacrifice for sin. This is one area they will always show commonality. If Satan can just accomplish this one thing (getting some to believe that Jesus is not God), then he has succeeded in keeping a lost person lost. Why? Because Jesus Christ and His atoning blood is the only way to God...the only way; there is no other. Jesus said that He was the way the truth and the life and that no man can come to the Father but by the Son. Any cult, false doctrine or false religion at its heart will go straight for the lie that Jesus is not the only way to God and that He is not God and will try to convince anyone who will listen that these lies are true. If either of these lies were true we would have no way to God and Satan knows it. This is his aim. There had to be a perfect sacrifice for sin and God is the only perfect sacrifice. If Jesus were not God, then sin could not be atoned for and this is Satan's main focus. Only a pure and spotless Lamb could atone for sin and Jesus Christ, God in the flesh, is that only spotless Lamb who could accomplish salvation for a lost people. Without God, in the form of His sinless Son, there is no salvation.

    The entire Word of God has one truth threaded throughout. It is this: God created man in His image, but because of the desire to be self ruling, man, through Adam, sinned against God. God, knowing this would happen before it did, provided a way for man to be reconciled to Himself. It involved a perfect sacrifice. Only the blood of a sinless sacrifice could pay the debt man owed to God because of his sin. This perfect sacrifice would be God Himself, in the form of His Son, Jesus Christ. It is Christ's blood shed on the cross at Calvary that paid our debt; and because He rose from the dead and ascended into Heaven, we who believe in Him will also be resurrected to everlasting life with God. If we will believe on Him and what He said He did and give our lives to Him, we will be saved and therefore reconciled to God.

The Word of God says that it is by grace, through faith that we are saved and that not of ourselves or our works lest we should boast (Ephesians 2:8-9). We have no part in salvation but to receive it.

This is the simple and only gospel of God. Christ died for our sins and it is only through Him that a man can be saved. Satan is behind all who deny this truth. And this is what the Jehovah's Witnesses do. They deny the Deity of Christ and call Him someone else. On this one point they are vehement. Christ is not God, they say. So who then are they witnessing for? It is not for Jehovah, but for one who disguises himself as Jehovah; and that is Satan...the enemy of God and of our souls. Satan has always wanted to be God and his desire is that he can get vulnerable and deceived souls to follow his lies. Then they will be worshiping him. They will think they are worshiping Jehovah but in truth will be worshiping Satan who is disguising himself.

Chapter Three

Identifying the Counterfeit

I heard someone say that the way a bank teller easily recognizes counterfeit money and distinguishes the real from the fake is by knowing very well what the true money looks like. She doesn't study all fake money but rather studies the real thing. When a counterfeit bill comes to her she will easily recognize that it is counterfeit because she knows the real money so well. This should be the way we recognize lies that come to our door or come to us in any other way…by knowing the true Word of God so well that we know when it is not being spoken.

So many people who have become believers have not bothered to study God's Word, even though we are exhorted to be ready in an instant to explain what we believe and why…to preach sound doctrine and to rebuke and reprove false doctrine (2 Timothy 4:2). Therefore, they are not armed to refute what Jehovah's Witnesses claim as truth. They are not in danger if they are truly believers because they are sealed with the Holy Spirit unto salvation (Eph. 4:30, Jn 3:16, Jn 10:9,28, Romans 11:29, Heb. 6:4-6, 10:38-39, 1 Jn 2:19, Acts 13:48), but they are really helpless to refute what this group claims. Jehovah's Witnesses are very well prepared to indoctrinate the lost with their lies. So well prepared are they that I would admonish anyone who is visited by them to kindly dismiss them and not invite them into your house unless you are clearly led by the Holy Spirit to do so.

I have been moved by the Lord, as I said earlier, to write this book called "Whose Witnesses?" Since then I have been strangely visited by no less than twenty (could be more) people claiming to be speaking God's truth, calling themselves Jehovah's Witnesses. Now, my family has moved since God has put this on my heart and somehow at each location the doorbell rings, and there stand on my porch, those who believe they are spreading God's truth but are not.

I have been led to engage them because I felt the Lord has prepared me to and I also have a heavy heart for their deceived state. I want to at least speak to them the true way to salvation and possibly plant a seed of truth in their hearts. But I will tell you that the scripture as always is right on. "Don't invite them in." Now I have a very soft heart for the lost and deceived. Of course like everyone else at some point, I was once lost and deceived as well. My heart clings to God's and feels just what He does for the lost...I desire that none perish, but that all would come to the saving knowledge of Christ. I desire that the truth would be rightly spoken through me and that my light would shine to those in the dark, showing them the way also. But this group is different. I really believe that and the Word warns us of that. We should not engage them lightly. They are highly skilled and have been trained very craftily to address every sound scripture we might present to them with twisted doctrine, circular logic and half truths.

> Their motive is not to lead you to salvation.
> Their motive is not to save the lost.
> Their motive is not to bless others with life and truth and healing.
> Their motive is not to comfort the hurting.

Their motive is not to feed the hungry.
It is not to care for the fatherless or the widow.
It is not to visit the imprisoned, or bring hope to the hopeless.
It is not to make the blind to see or the deaf to hear.
It is not to bind-up the brokenhearted or to set the captives free.

Their motive is not even to love the Lord our God with all their heart and with all their soul and with all their mind, nor is it to love their neighbor as themselves. And it is absolutely not to "know nothing but Jesus Christ and Him crucified". No. It is none of these things.

Their sole motive is to convince anyone they can that Jesus Christ is not God. Basically, that's it. And that if you want to be one of the 144,000 who are saved through the Great Tribulation, then you must become a good Jehovah's Witness. And I know who is behind that message; it is Satan.

So even though I know that God wants us to witness to all people, it is wise to pray for them and leave it at that. God will bring many Jehovah's Witnesses to the truth. I am not saying that they are beyond hope; not at all. What I am saying is that the Word tells us that this false gospel that they are pushing is directly from the spirit of antichrist. Our strongest weapon here is prayer.

Jesus said in John 10 that His sheep know His voice and will not follow another. Though another may call them, they will not go with a stranger. They hear and follow only The Good Shepherd; the Lord Jesus Christ.

Chapter Four

What the Witnesses Believe

I guess it is necessary to touch on what the Jehovah's Witnesses believe. I am not interested in and I don't think it's necessary to pick apart their doctrine bit by bit. Why? Because we can easily establish with a few major beliefs of theirs that they know not the heart of God nor the truth that He has spoken in His Word.

If we do an internet search on the Jehovah's Witnesses, one of the first hits is from the popular Wikipedia site. The first thing that is said about this group is that they are a Christian denomination. But that is false. They are absolutely not a Christian denomination. In fact, they fully deny the Christ of the Bible and claim He is someone who He is not. As many faults as the denominations have, and they have many, they all agree on one basic truth and that is the truth that Jesus Christ is God in the flesh and died for the sin of mankind, was resurrected from the dead and ascended into Heaven in glory, and that He is the only way to God.

To be considered Christian, this foundational truth at the very least must be embraced fully. The Jehovah's Witnesses do not embrace this, and not only that…they vehemently deny it, and therefore are not Christian. They preach another gospel.

They claim that they follow the Word of God but they have their own Bible translation (The New World Translation) that has been doctored and changed throughout so that a lot of the scriptures refuting their denial of Christ are missing or reworded. They mostly get their "truth" from a publication of theirs called "The Watchtower", which is full of false doctrine and is contrary to the true Word of God.

They want to quickly establish that the name of God is Jehovah, which it is, and that some other names used in the Bible for God are referring to someone else and not God. But we know that God Himself has given Himself many names. All of these names are descriptive of His nature but they are still His names. He is LORD, He is Lord, Yahweh, Jehovah God, Jehovah Jireh, Jehovah Nisi, El-Shaddai, Elohim, Adonai, I AM and dozens more. We also know from Psalm 138 that God exalts His Word **ABOVE** His name. I'll say it again…God exalts His Word **ABOVE** His name.

We can prove very quickly with just a few scriptures that the Jehovah's Witnesses ignore the Bible's clear teaching that Jesus is not only the Son of God but that He IS God… He said so Himself. But they have craftily (which is Satan's way) twisted key scriptures to try and explain away the glaring and inescapable truth that Jesus IS God and must be God if He is to save mankind from himself. It is not enough to believe that Jesus is the Son of God. He is the Son of God but more than that…**He is God the Son.**

The Jehovah's Witnesses also claim that they are the 144,000 spoken of in the book of Revelation. But this number represents the twelve tribes of Israel. The Witnesses claim that they are spiritual Israel. There is a term for that and it is "Replacement Theology". This false doctrine claims that the church has replaced Israel (clearly refuted over and over again in the Word; God has two flocks…the church, consisting of Jew and Gentile and the nation of Israel that will come to know the true Messiah during the Great Tribulation period). But the Witnesses believe they are the 144,000 spoken of in the book of Revelation. They are not. There are no lost tribes of Israel. All the faithful from the north migrated south to Judah where the temple was (Chuck Missler's commentaries, 2 Chronicles 11:16).

Another major point of the Witnesses is this: They say there is no Trinity. They say that God cannot be a triune God. But they say this because they can't understand the concept and not because it is what the Word teaches. Because the Word teaches us that God is three in one. **God is distinctly three yet He remains one.**

They believe many more unscriptural things that are found nowhere in the Word of God. But the main belief is that Jesus is not God and that is what I will focus on. It would take deep exposition and lengthy discussion to refute all of their false claims and many have done that and I praise God that He has anointed many to do just that. But He has placed it on my heart to do this one thing: I will show anyone who reads this book that the Word of God undeniably and overwhelmingly says that Jesus Christ and Jehovah are one. This one truth causes the Witnesses' doctrine to turn to dust. They have no religion if Jesus Christ is God and He is! Jesus Christ is Jehovah. He is the Son and yet the Word shows us that He is Jehovah. This is a concept that must be received rather than understood but it is truth nonetheless.

I can't argue this point with much clarity on my own so I won't try but there is one thing I can do…I can point to what the Word says…that I can do. The rest is in God, the Holy Spirit's hands. And He is quite capable of showing us that this idea, that He is one God yet in three persons, is absolutely true and must be true whether we understand it or not. The scriptures speak for themselves. After all, "the Word of God is quick and powerful, and sharper than any two-edged sword, piercing even unto the dividing asunder of soul and spirit, and of joints and marrow, and is a discerner of the thoughts and intents of the heart" (Hebrews 4:12).

Chapter Five

Who Does Jesus Say He Is?

Alright...we know then that the Jehovah's Witness's main and vehement claim is that Jesus Christ is not God. The most effective way to refute this is to check-out who Jesus says He is. So I want to begin this chapter by stating who God says He is through His Word. Not only are we going to see that He is one God, but that He is three persons in one...the Trinity. The Godhead is composed of three persons. He is God the Father, God the Son and God the Holy Spirit...all at once. In the same way He is three yet one, we who are made in His image are also comprised of three but remain one. We know from the Word that we are made up of body, soul and spirit. Each part of our being has different functions yet we are still only one. The body is the part of us that is the physical, visible me. The soul is the part of me that is the seat of my will and my emotions. My spirit is that part of me that can know God.

I think this is a good analogy but it still falls short. This is why: The Word teaches us that God is distinctly three persons yet is one God. We have to hold this truth as truth because the Word teaches it. It is not scriptural to melt all three persons of the Godhead into one whereby causing Father, Son and Holy Spirit to disappear. Remember that God is three distinct persons yet is one God. This is a glorious mystery. The simple heart will receive it and not try to dissect it.

Now let me add this thought: While it is unscriptural to melt all three persons of the Godhead into one without holding at the same time the truth that God is three yet one, it is just as unscriptural to think of one person of the Godhead as being in any way separate or in individual operation apart from the other two. When we see Jesus Christ...Father and Spirit are there as well. When we see Father God, Jehovah... God the Spirit and God the Son are there as well...they are never separate...they are one. When we see the Holy Spirit... Father God and God the Son are present...always.

There are cults, and churches involved in false teaching, that do this. Some may focus exclusively on Father God and treat the Son and the Holy Spirit as if they are less than God...this is false teaching. There are some who focus so heavily on the Holy Spirit that Jesus is rarely mentioned and this actually causes the Holy Spirit to appear as someone less than Almighty God...which He is not. This leans towards idol worship. He is equally God with the Father and Son. There are some denominations that focus exclusively on Jesus Christ and exclude Jehovah God and treat the Holy Spirit as if He is less than God or someone to stay away from because He is spooky. But the Word of God teaches that each person of the triune Godhead is God...each is equally God with the Father and we will see that as we travel through the Word in this short book.

Let's pay close attention as we go through the Word. There are wonderful surprises waiting to be discovered if we will look for them. We will see that God often speaks of Himself interchangeably as Father, Son and Spirit, and we will see that this is intentional on the part of God. I believe His purpose for doing it is to illustrate for us that He is indeed three yet one. Let's notice how He never attempts to explain this hard truth to us, or even to convince us of it...He just states it all through His Word and asks us to believe it. How great is God!

Let's begin in Genesis and move through the Bible and discover who God says He is. I will start by saying that I am going to use what most good scholars believe is the most accurate Bible translation, the King James Version. Here's why: It is a word for word translation of the oldest remaining texts and is not a paraphrased translation. It is translated from the most numerable and accurate transcripts. You can do a simple internet search on this for yourself so I won't get into it here. Most other translations are paraphrased, and while many of them are good, they miss some of the very important truths of God's Word. The King James Version is probably the best English translation we have so that is what I'll use. It is by no means perfect, but it is the most accurate.

Now I am no scholar so I want to make it clear that I am simply expressing in my own words what I have found that the Word clearly teaches about God. I am a serious Bible student but I am not attempting to set forth a highly organized and systematic exposition of theology on this topic. I am just going to write what I feel the Holy Spirit is putting on my heart to write and going to the scriptures He leads me to.

I'll begin by saying this: I am really just going to list many things God says about Himself. As I come to certain points, I may jump to many other parts in the Word which confirm these very points. Or, I may backtrack to connect to something I have already said. I am going to try and stick to scriptures that show us who God is, who His Son is and who the Holy Spirit is; and that each time we see one mentioned it is in a sense speaking of all three persons of the Godhead. They are three in one. Jehovah God is our triune God and the Word proves that.

I want to encourage the reader to follow along with a KJV of the Bible and to look the scriptures up as we go. I say this because the KJV is the one I will use and I will point out some very important points that may not be in a different translation. Some paraphrased translations leave out subtle things that are very important.

This is not an easy reading book but is a book that intends to encourage the reader to search the Word hard. I truly believe that if we set our hearts to know truth, and search the scriptures, then as we see the Word and read the Word, something supernatural will happen to us...we will be washed in the water by the Word (Ephesians 5:26) and the Holy Spirit will make truth known to us.

"And you will seek Me and find Me, when you search for Me with all your heart" (Jeremiah 29:13).

In the Beginning God...

Alright...the very first reference to God in the Word is found in Genesis 1:1 where we read, "In the beginning God created the heaven and the earth." The Hebrew word for God here is Elohim which is PLURAL! (Chuck Missler's commentary on Genesis) So, the very first reference to our ONE God is used in a singular context with a plural meaning. AMAZING! God opens His Word to us in astonishing power, establishing right away that He is one God but in three persons. He is God...Elohim. If this is the first thing He establishes then it must be mighty important, don't you think? It is.

Now, in verse 26 we read that God says, "Let **US** make man in **OUR** image. Then, in verse 27 God is almost summarizing what He just said. But this time He says, "So God created man in **HIS** own image." He is telling us that when He said **OUR** image and **HIS** image, He meant the same thing. He is restating that He is one God but in three persons.

Alright, now let's skip to the first time we hear God give Himself another very important name. And it is His name and not just a description. In Exodus 3:14 we see that God tells Moses that His name is "I AM". Now this is extremely important because it is a name that Jesus will also use of Himself; so I want to skip to the gospel of John for a minute and look at something absolutely amazing.

John 18:5 & 6 records the arrest of Jesus. When the band of men and chief officers came to the garden, Jesus asked them who it was they were seeking. They said they were looking for Jesus of Nazareth and His response to them in the original Greek text is this: "I AM." The King James Version and other translations add the word "He" for clarity, but it does not belong there. Jesus said simply, "I AM". And it is written in all capital letters just like it is in Exodus. Then His captors were blown down. Jesus Christ gave Himself God's most powerful, all encompassing and absolute name, "I AM". This is one of the most obvious events in the entire Bible where Jesus Christ claims to be God, but there are many others.

It is also very important to know that the whole reason that these men wanted to crucify Jesus is because He claimed to be God. It is very clear in the Bible that Jesus' own proclamation is that He is God in the flesh. This is why the Jews crucified Him...He said He was God and they hated Him for it. But let's move on. A side-note here: While it was the Jews who crucified Jesus they were simply acting out pre-determined truth. Jesus had to go to the cross if sin was to be forgiven...He laid His life down willingly and no man took it from Him. It is our sin that required it so all mankind is guilty for crucifying Jesus, not just the Jews. And remember that it pleased the Father to bruise His Son so that mankind could be reconciled to God.

Now I want to reiterate that I am writing what the Holy Spirit is leading me to write. These are references that stand out to me personally. There are so many more that I will not get to. That being said, let's skip to Deuteronomy 32.

In verse 15 we see that God calls Himself the "Rock of his salvation" (Israel's salvation). Then He continues and says that this "Rock" is the one who formed Israel. Let's skip to the New Testament where it is understood that Jesus is also called "Rock". In 1 Corinthians 10:4, we see Paul explaining that the "Rock" in the wilderness with the Jews who was God, was none other than Jesus Christ. Just think about that for a minute. We can see that the term "rock" in the Old Testament also referred to Christ who was to come.

In the Beginning Was the Word

Now in the gospel of John, we see that John introduces Jesus as the "Word". He says that "In the beginning was the Word, and the Word was with God, and the Word was God. The same was in the beginning with God. All things were made by Him; and without Him was not anything made that was made. In Him was life; and the life was the light of men. And the light shines in the darkness; and the darkness comprehended it not." Wow! This is an amazing passage that reveals so much. Let's look at a couple of very important points that John establishes right off the bat. First, we see that the "Word" is definitely Jesus Christ. This is whom John's whole gospel is about and he introduces Him to us here as the "Word". John tells us that the Word (Jesus) was in the beginning with God and that He was God. Then John tells us that the Word made everything that was made. In other words...Jesus Christ made **ALL** things. **He is Creator God!!! Yes! He is Creator God.** Look at John 1:14: John says that this same Word who he has called God was made flesh and dwelt among us. Well, we know who was made flesh and dwelt among us...Jesus Christ; and John says he is God and creator God at that. Now, if that were not enough, John goes on to tell us that Jesus is the light that shines in the darkness.

Ok...let's go back to Genesis 1 where we see that God said, "Let there be light" and there was, and it shone in the darkness. Again...Jesus is God and John is establishing that. We can clearly see that Genesis 1 and John 1 are parallel scriptures...they say the same thing. In Genesis it is Jehovah God we are introduced to. In John it is Jesus Christ we are introduced to and they are one in the same.

Jesus Christ is Jehovah God. There is no escaping it. While we have three persons of the Godhead; Father, Son and Holy Spirit, we have one...Almighty God.

Oh...there is one last point on this scripture. John said that Jesus was the light and that the darkness comprehended it not. It is darkness that does not comprehend Jesus; and Satan is the prince of that darkness.

In Deuteronomy 32:30, Moses is calling Jehovah God both "Rock" and "LORD" in the same breath. Jesus Christ is also called "Rock" and "Lord". The name "Lord" is used in lower case letters here (except the L) to differentiate between God the Father and God the Son. When it is God the Father who is being spoken of, the name is spelled with all caps. They are still one. Later we will see that Jesus is also called LORD.

Now look at Deuteronomy 32:39 & 40 with me for a minute. God is saying here that He alone is God and there is no god with Him. Then He says that He kills and makes alive; He wounds and He heals. Then He says that He lives forever.

Let's jump to Revelation 1:18. We see here that it is Jesus Christ who says He lives for evermore. Also...go back a few verses in Revelation 1. Revelation 1: 8, 11 and 17 say this: "I am Alpha and Omega; the beginning and the ending" and "I am Alpha and Omega; the first and the last" and "I am the first and the last". Then Jesus continues on in Revelation 1:18 saying that not only is He the first and the last (that which is only true of Jehovah God) but that He is the one who "lives and was dead; and behold, I am alive for evermore." Jesus is clearly establishing the truth that He is God. He really shocks us by declaring that not only is He the Alpha and Omega (a title only given to Jehovah God) but that He was alive, dead, then alive again for evermore!

This is what the Jehovah's Witnesses don't like. They say that Jesus could not be God because God can't die and Jesus said He was dead, but alive again. But this truth is inescapable. Jesus Himself is not only declaring absolutely that He is God but that He was crucified as God and was resurrected as God and remains God for evermore. Now any religion that wants to deny Christ's Deity MUST conclude that Jesus Christ is a lunatic and cannot be trusted or believed. Jesus tells us right here that these things are true of Him. He is God and He was crucified as God. No one and nothing but God could pay our sin debt on that cross; only God in the flesh...Jesus Christ. Oh, if we will open our mouths wide, He will fill them (Psalm 81:10). God Almighty is not only the Sovereign of the Universe but He is the spotless Lamb slain before the foundation of the world... "If you will receive it" (Matthew 11:14).

And it is something that must be received rather than fully understood. The Word tells us overwhelmingly that there is one God but that He is made up of three persons and these three cannot be separated. They are always together in perfect agreement and never operate independently of one another. It is impossible to say that God is anything but one God, and it is impossible to say that He is anything but three persons in one Godhead. Both ideas must be held at once as truth.

God is Father but He is also the Son who became incarnate and dressed Himself in flesh in order to identify with mankind...fallen mankind. And even more than that, He came in the flesh so that He could be formed inside of the believer by the supernatural work and presence of the Holy

Spirit, replacing the sinful, self-ruling nature of the first Adam with the perfect nature of the Last Adam...Jesus Christ. This is a great mystery.

God is Father and Son but He is also the Holy Spirit who comes and indwells the believer and gives us the power to live for God and to please God...He counsels us in the ways of God...He directs our paths. He forms Christ in us who will believe.

I guess if I had to really over-emphasize something in this book it is this: The truth of who God is, is both very simple and very complex. He has said that His ways are higher than our ways (Isaiah 55:9) and His ways are unsearchable and beyond finding out (Romans 11:33). So here is the thing we must just accept because the Word says it: God is three persons but one God. As I said earlier, I will show using the Word of God, how each person of the Godhead is referred to interchangeably as God, and that this is by design. God wants to emphasize the absolute necessity of knowing and receiving that He is three yet one. We cannot know Him if we don't accept this one thing as truth because all truth hinges on this fact. Salvation is dependent upon Jesus Christ being God the Son. Satan knows this, like I said earlier, and that is why he attacks it.

In order to know Christ and who He is we must understand that He is Almighty God who made Himself flesh in the form of Jesus Christ the Son who has always been and will always be. We must understand that the Holy Spirit is a person and not a vapor or essence or power of God. He is the person of the Godhead, equally God with the Father and with the Son who comes to live inside of us and leads us in ways of righteousness for His name's sake.

God Will Provide Himself a Lamb

Alright now my thoughts are going back to Genesis where we read the account of Abraham leading Isaac up to be sacrificed. This is so important. Let's linger here for a minute. The story is found in Genesis 22. Abraham is leading Isaac, his beloved son who was the promise of God to Abraham...a great treasure to his heart, up a hill where Abraham would follow God's instructions to slay Isaac. Isaac begins to notice that there is no lamb to slay and asks his father where the lamb is. Then the next thing that happens is astounding and it is a pattern for what God had planned since the beginning of time. Abraham says: "God will provide Himself a lamb..."

Abraham is prophesying here. He may or may not have known it. We read in Hebrews that he did know that God was going to do something miraculous and either stop the slaying or resurrect Isaac. But I don't know if he really understood the full magnitude at that point (maybe he did) of his words "God will provide Himself". Look at that closely: Chuck Missler asks in his study on this event, and I agree with him, if God is telling us here in a hidden way that God Himself would be the ultimate sacrifice in the form of His only begotten Son, Jesus Christ? I say yes! He is! God would be the sacrifice. And indeed He was. Only God could pay our debt for sin; our good works never could do it...never could and never can.

Now there is a very curious event in the book of Judges that I want to mention even though I could be wrong. It is curious and the reader can decide for himself if it is too big a stretch but let's look at it anyway.

We all know who Samson is, right? Well, his story begins in Judges 13. We see that his parents were visited by someone called simply "a man of God", and also called "the angel of the LORD". He brings them the message of the soon to come birth of their son Samson. Without getting into details I just want to mention a very curious part of this story. We are led to believe, and then it is confirmed in my opinion to the serious student of the Word, that this visitor is actually God. He, in my opinion, is presenting Himself here in a visible form, and that visible form is the Lord Jesus Christ Himself.

Scholars call pre-incarnate appearances of Christ in the Bible a "Christophany". This has to be one of them and I'll tell you why. Samson's parents offer worship before this "angel of the LORD" and he accepts it! An angel would never accept worship, never. But this messenger does. He states at first that only God can be worshiped, but that is just perfect evidence that He is telling them then that He is not just any messenger but that He is God.

The "angel" is saying that if it is true that only God can be worshiped, and I am receiving that worship, then I must be God. They both recognize that after he has departed anyway, when they say to themselves: "How is it that we have not died?"

They ask this because they know they have just seen God in a visible form ...the pre-incarnate Christ, to be exact.

The Father is invisible and no man has ever seen Him except the Son, and this was well-known. But they know that they HAVE seen Him and have not died. That is because it is God the Son who they saw and He is visible. It is a very mysterious portion of scripture and a lot of fun to study and I won't get into any more here but it is important to establish the point because I want to then look at what name He gives Himself.

When Samson's mother asks what His name is, His response is fascinating! LISTEN...This "messenger" says, "Why do you ask my name seeing that it is WONDERFUL?" (NKJ) Now skip to Isaiah 9 for a minute where the prophet (probably my favorite one) is telling us about this Messiah to come. As I am writing this I am singing it because it is the scripture that inspired Handel's Messiah Hallelujah Chorus. "And His name shall be called WONDERFUL, Counselor, The Mighty God, The Everlasting Father, The Prince of Peace..." Hal..le..lu..jah, hallelujah, hallelujah...hal..le..lu..jah!

That "messenger" who came to Samson's mother was the one and only Jehovah God in the pre-incarnate form of His Son Jesus Christ who is the second person of the Trinity and His name is WONDERFUL!

Other translations wrongly leave out a comma at the end of Wonderful and call Him Wonderful Counselor...which He is, but no...this is just WONDERFUL all by itself. I love it! Actually, I believe that there is no punctuation in Hebrew like we have in English so I am guessing that this was added to clarify that there is a separation intended in the Hebrew. But other, less accurate translations take liberty here and group two words together that perhaps shouldn't be.

If Almighty God did not come to us in the form of that glorious babe in a manger, then we would have no remedy for our sin. It took the holy blood of Creator God, Jehovah, in the form of Christ on that cross at Calvary to atone for our sin. Nothing else could do it. And all of this was "...foreordained before the foundation of the world, but was manifest in these last times for you..." (1 Peter 1:20).

This is glorious redemption; the glorious impossible; too confounding to think of. So confounding is it as a matter of fact that it must be received by the heart and not the head in order to understand it. It is the greatest gift of pure and holy love that could ever be given. And it is a promise that belongs to all who will just humbly receive it. What kind of love is this? Thank You Father.

Let's backtrack for a minute and look at an event in Joshua that also has to be a pre-incarnate appearance of Christ. It is found in Joshua 5:13-15. Joshua runs into a "man" standing in front of him who is holding a sword. Joshua asks whose side He is on and He says that He is on neither side but that

He is captain of the host of the LORD. With that, Joshua falls prostrate before Him and WORSHIPS Him. This is a pre-incarnate appearance of Jesus Christ. But look at what happens next: Joshua is told by this captain of the host of the LORD to take off his shoes for the land he is standing on is holy. Does this sound familiar? It should because Almighty God, the Great I AM, said the exact thing to Moses when Moses approached the burning bush where God was. Why were both places holy? Because Jehovah God was there! This scripture not only proves it is God who was speaking to both men but that it was Christ and that Christ existed in glory before He came in the flesh (John 17:5), and that He and the Father are one. Remember that it was foreordained before the foundation of the world that God would become flesh in the form of Jesus Christ the Son and offer Himself as a sacrifice for sinful mankind.

"Earth's crammed with heaven and every bush is ablaze with the fire of God but only him who sees takes off his shoes."
Elizabeth Barrett Browning

Look at 2 Samuel 23:2, we see that the Holy Spirit spoke. This means He must be a person and not just an essence or vapor, like the Witnesses claim. The Jehovah's Witnesses try to force the Spirit of God to be an essence or force so they can squeeze in their doctrine of denying the three persons of God whereby denying that Christ is God in the flesh. If they admit that the Holy Spirit is a person then they have to admit that Jesus is God like He claims. This is because if God can be one God but also comprised of two persons, then certainly He could be one God comprised of three persons like the Bible says He is.

In Job 33:4 we see that Elihu, a mysterious person in the Word, speaks to Job and says that the Spirit of God made him. Wait a minute! I thought Jehovah God made all things!

That's what Genesis and the rest of the Word teaches us. But wait another minute! John tells us as does Paul and probably many others I'm not recalling right now, that Jesus Christ made ALL things. So then, we have Father God claiming to have made all things, the Spirit of God made Elihu, and Jesus Christ made all things that are made and that NOTHING was made apart from Him. Beautiful! Isn't God so wonderful to show us this? God is three in one. He is Father, Holy Spirit and Son...God.

Now the Psalms are full of the revelation of Christ as God if we will look closely. Here are a few references that jump out at me. In Psalm 23 we see that the LORD (Jehovah God, Father God) is the Shepherd of His people and He cares for them as precious treasures. Well, we know that Jesus Christ is the Good Shepherd who does all these things we read of in this Psalm.

Who Is This King of Glory?

Then we can look at Psalm 24 and see that the earth and all that is in it is the LORD's (Jehovah's). Well, we know that John tells us that Jesus Christ created all things and that they belong to Him. In Revelation we see that Jesus owns and rules over the heavens and the earth.

Then David asks a question and answers it. First he says, "Who is this King of glory?" Then he answers his own question by saying that He is "The LORD strong and mighty, the LORD mighty in battle" (Psalm 24:8). Well, Revelation presents this King of glory to us and He is Jesus Christ who is strong and mighty and mighty in battle. This is Jesus Christ who is being referred to here as well as Jehovah God because they are the same. But look: LORD is used and it is Jesus. We know when LORD is used it is Jehovah God. Jesus is Jehovah God.

"One thing have I desired of the LORD, that will I seek after; that I may dwell in the house of the LORD all the days of my life, to behold the beauty of the LORD, and to inquire in His temple" (Psalm 27:4).

Jesus said that the whole Word is written of Him (Hebrews 10:7). Just listen to the curious tone in that question: "Who is this King of glory?" It is the mystery that God kept secret until Messiah's birth. This King of glory would be revealed in the form of a helpless babe, and that babe would be God Himself in the flesh; the Messiah...born for the express purpose of dying for your sin and mine.

Psalm 50 is a very provocative Psalm. It is written by Asaph and seems to prophesy of Christ's Second Coming. It opens with profound revelation that Christ is God. Listen: It says, "The mighty God, even the LORD..." Now look at Isaiah 9:6 where the prophet announces just who this coming Messiah is and what He shall be called. "His name shall be called Wonderful, Counselor, THE MIGHTY GOD..." This is Jehovah God who is coming in the flesh as Jesus and His name shall be called The Mighty God! Wow, how great is that? There is more in this verse in Isaiah but I will come to that a little later; let's move on.

Now look at what is being said here in Psalm 50. It is describing God as The Mighty God (A name given to Jesus Christ) as He calls the earth from the rising of the sun to the setting thereof. He says that out of Zion (Israel) God has shined (meaning God in the form of His Messiah, Jesus). Asaph is saying that out of Zion, God will come. He says, "Our God shall come, and shall not keep silence: a fire shall devour before Him, and it shall be very tempestuous round about Him. He shall call to the heavens from above, and to the earth, that He may judge His people."

Well, we know that Jesus Christ is the one who judges at the end of Armageddon, and then again at the end of the thousand year reign at the Great White Throne Judgment of the wicked. Jesus said while He was still in the flesh and before His ascension that He did not come to judge the world but to save it (John 12:47) and that the Father alone judges. Then we will see that Jesus is the judge and that the Father does not judge (Matthew 5:22). But this only intensifies the truth that Jesus is God. This is because we know that when Christ Jesus said that He did not come to judge, He was referring to His mission as the Son of God; God in the flesh when He came to save. Oh, but when He returns at the Second Coming, at Armageddon, He comes as judge and devours with fire (remember He said that He wished this fire were already kindled; He longs for this day...Luke 12:49). We know absolutely from Revelation that Jesus is the one who comes with a devouring fire and sits on the throne of God as judge over all creation. Romans and 2 Corinthians both speak of this Judgment Seat of Christ. Only God judges... Jesus is God.

We see that in Psalm 145:13 that David is speaking of God's kingdom and says it is an everlasting kingdom. Now look at Luke 23:42 where the thief who is hanging on a cross next to Christ says, "Lord, remember me when You come into Your kingdom."

This is the same kingdom of God, and it is Christ's kingdom. Christ Jesus is God. In Psalm 147:3 we read that God is the one who heals the brokenhearted and binds up their wounds. Well, look at Luke 4:21. It is Jesus Christ who heals the brokenhearted and binds up their wounds.

Psalm 146:6 tells us that it is God who made all things; the heavens, the earth and all that is in them. Now look again at John 1:10-14. John tells us again that Jesus made the world. In fact, as I mentioned earlier, Jesus made all that was made and nothing that was made was made apart from Him. Verse 10 says that the world was made by Jesus, and the world knew Him not. Anyone who does not receive who Jesus said He is (Almighty God) is of the world...the world knows Him not. But He says in verse 12 that those who do receive Him have been given power to become the sons of God. Then verse 14 says that the Word (Jesus Christ) was made flesh and dwelt among us.

Ok. If we know that this Word is Jesus, which we do know by this passage, then we also know that this Word is God and that He created all things and that not only did He create all things but He was made flesh (in the form of the second person of the Trinity) and dwelt among us. Jesus Christ is God made flesh to dwell among us and to die on the cross at Calvary in payment for all sin, was resurrected and then ascended to Heaven and sits at the right hand of God (Jesus is God's righteous right arm).

Psalm 148:5 says that God commanded and they (all things) were created. This is Jesus because we know that Jesus Christ created anything that was made. Look at Malachi 2:10: "Has not one God created us?" The answer is yes…only one God created us.

Well, now we have come to one of my most favorite books in the entire Bible and that is Song of Songs. I believe that this is an allegory of the church and Jesus Christ. But more than that I believe it is an allegory of the individual believer and Jesus Christ as bride and Bridegroom. It is a study on the intimate relationship with our Creator, the Lord Jesus, that we are entitled to as believers. It is a song that rejoices in the delights of this spiritual marriage. Without getting into any more details I really just want to say one thing about this book. The Bridegroom is the Lord Jesus Christ and the bride is each believer who has given himself fully to God. God always refers to Himself as the Husband and believers as either the bride (who is the church) or the wife (who is Israel).

Jesus has two flocks. One is the church or the bride and the other is Israel or the wife of God. They will be made one flock in the end, we read in John 10:16. This is another topic that I won't get into here any more than to say that there is one flock that is the bride of Christ (both Jew and Gentile) and another flock who will come to Christ during the Great Tribulation period. These are the 144,000 Jews spoken of in Revelation...these are not Jehovah's Witnesses, like the Witnesses claim. This is a misunderstanding of the Word of God.

The seven year Tribulation period taught in Daniel and in so many other places in the Word is also called the time of Jacob's trouble. This is a period of refining for Israel that completes 70 weeks of years that God determined against her to finish her transgression (Daniel 9:24). 69 of them have already occurred and then an undetermined period of time is elapsing while God is gathering the church...we are in that period...the church age. Israel has been blinded in part until the fullness of the gentiles is come in (Romans 11:25) because they, as a nation, rejected Christ as the Messiah when He presented Himself to them as such. When the church is complete (the fullness of the gentiles) then Israel as a nation will be un-blinded and receive her Messiah at last. It is during this period of time that ALL Israel will be saved. This means that a remnant of every tribe of Israel (there are no lost tribes; 2 Chr. 11:16) will be brought to know Christ Jesus as their Messiah, their God and Savior. These are the 144,000. They are not the church nor are they the Witnesses.

I Saw Also the Lord Sitting Upon a Throne, High and Lifted Up...

In Isaiah 2:4 we learn that it is God who judges nations. In Revelation we learn that Jesus Christ is the one who judges all nations. Isaiah 2:11-17 tells us that God ALONE will be exalted in that day (the Day of the LORD). Well, Revelation clearly tells us that in this same day (the Day of the LORD) Jesus Christ is exalted as KING OF KINGS AND LORD

OF LORDS. In Isaiah 2:19 we are told that people will hide in the rocks from His (Jesus') majesty when He shall arise to shake the earth. Isaiah is at the same time speaking of Jehovah God and prophesying of Jesus Christ in the Day of the LORD. They are one in the same. Jesus Christ is Jehovah God.

Now in Isaiah 6 we see that Isaiah sees a vision of God, seated on the throne and His train filled the temple. The Seraphims are above it and cry, "holy, holy, holy is the LORD of hosts..." (Isaiah 6:3). Then Isaiah cries "Woe is me! For I am undone...mine eyes have seen the King, the LORD of hosts..." (Isaiah 6:5). Isaiah is responding to what he has just seen in Isaiah 6:1. He saw the Lord on His throne (Lord, not LORD) meaning Jehovah God. But then when he speaks in verse 5 He says LORD and not Lord. This is intentional to show the interchangeability of the Godhead. The Holy Spirit is showing us that Jesus is God.

The prophet Isaiah says in chapter 12 that Israel will in that day praise God as their salvation. Verse 2 says that JEHOVAH is their strength and their song. We know that Jesus said He is salvation. In fact He says that He is the ONLY way to salvation. He said that He is the way, the truth and the life and that no man can come to the Father but by Him. We are also told that anyone who calls upon the name of the Lord (this is the Lord Jesus Christ who is being referenced here) shall be saved.

We see here in this same 12th chapter of Isaiah that the Holy One of Israel is referenced. That brings me to another series of scriptures concerning who this Holy One is. Let's look for a minute at Psalm 16. David is crying out to God concerning himself but then something changes in verse 10. David is prophesying in Messiah's voice as he does in Psalm 22 and elsewhere. He says: "For Thou will not leave my soul in hell; neither will Thou suffer Thy Holy One to see corruption." This is Jesus who is the Holy One. And we know that there is only one Holy One…God. But it doesn't end there.

Luke records Peter speaking on the day of Pentecost as he quotes David in Acts 2:27 where he repeats this prophecy and attributes it to Jesus Christ. In Acts 2:30-31 Luke explains this very thing so there is no conjecture here on my part. Luke explains that David, being a prophet, was prophesying of Jesus Christ (the Holy One) who would descend into hell in our place and then be resurrected to life, never seeing corruption. Hallelujah! Also, we see in Luke 4:34 that even the demons call Jesus the Holy One of God. They knew who He was, but the Jehovah's Witnesses do not even know that much. Even if they knew that much it still is a problem for them because just knowing who Jesus is does not bring salvation…trusting Him as Lord and Savior does, however. No works can save us. JUST BELIEVE. That will save you.

Isaiah 12:9 speaks of the LORD (notice that this is Jehovah God) in His fierce wrath at the Last Day, as He destroys the wicked in His anger. Well, we know that it is Jesus at His Second Coming who destroys the wicked in the fierceness of His wrath.

Let's skip to Isaiah 14 and be fascinated at the clarity of what is said here. The prophet Isaiah is speaking of both Israel (all those who migrated down to Judah) that will be going into captivity under Nebuchadnezzar and of Israel in the Last Day at His Second Coming. Look, he says that Israel will finally be at rest and the whole earth will sing at His coming. We call this His Second Coming because He came to us the first time in the manger as the Lamb. At His Second Coming we will see Him as Lion. He is the Lion and the Lamb.

Isaiah 16:5 speaks about God sitting on the Throne of David's tabernacle (in other words, the tabernacle that David received plans for, which is patterned after the true one in heaven) judging and hastening righteousness. This is Jesus. Jesus sits on the Throne of David.

Isaiah 19 speaks of Last Day events. Isaiah speaks of the LORD (Jehovah) riding on the clouds bringing destruction to nations in the Last Day. In that Day (the Last Day) He will cause Egypt to know God. This has to be the Last Day Isaiah is prophesying about, because we have not seen this yet. Egypt is a Muslim nation and does not know the one true God. Also, who comes riding on the clouds in this, the Last Day, to destroy the wicked on the earth? It is none other than Jesus Christ our Lord and God. Look at Isaiah 21:9: "Babylon is fallen, is fallen!" This is exactly what is exclaimed in Revelation at her destruction in the Last Day.

Now look at this passage: Isaiah 22:23 says this about Christ: "I (God the Father) will fasten Him as a nail in a firm place; and He shall be for a glorious throne to His Father's house". Then verse 24 says: "In that day, says the LORD of Hosts, shall the nail that is fastened in the sure place be removed, and be cut down, and fall; and the burden that was upon it shall be cut-off: for the LORD has spoken it." What a glorious, glorious account of our Lord's crucifixion. Jesus was nailed to a sure place where the burden of the sin of all mankind was laid upon Him. He was removed from the cross and fell and was cut-off from God as sin; all in our place. Remember, that Messiah would be cut-off; He would have no offspring to speak of according to the prophecy we will read in Isaiah 53 when we get there. This is breathtaking prophecy and will prove with the rest of the Word that this is God who was cut-off in our place.

We see in chapter 24 that the Last Day prophecy is continuing but is intermingled with the Babylonian captivity prophecy for Israel (all who were in Judah). Isaiah is prophesying of a time when the whole earth fades away. It is a future time when the earth is burned with fire and only a few men are left. This is interesting and important because if we can establish that this is indeed Last Day prophecy (and we have) then we can also conclude that it is the Lord Jesus who is judging and devouring. Isaiah says this is God.

In chapter 33, Isaiah is quoting David and says: "Who among us shall dwell with the devouring fire?" I love this Psalm! Then the Psalm says the righteous will see the King in His beauty. We know that this King is Jesus Christ who is the KING OF KINGS. Then we see in verse 22 that the LORD is King. If God is King and Jesus is the KING OF KINGS, then we know that Jesus is God. If God is The KING and Jesus THE KING OF KINGS then Jesus is more than Jehovah God and Jehovah God is under Him...but this is not so! The only other conclusion then is that Jesus and the Father are One...they are God the Father and God the Son....God.

"He thought it not robbery to be equal with God..." (Philippians 2:6).

Isaiah 40:13 says: "Who has directed the Spirit of the LORD, or as His counselor has taught Him?" The answer of course is that no one has taught Him or directed Him. Why? It is because He is God. And notice that Creator God, Jehovah, is now referred to as the Spirit!

Isaiah 41:14 speaks of God as Redeemer and the Holy One as being the same. Well, we know that Jesus Christ is the Redeemer and the Holy One. Romans 3:24 says that redemption is from Christ. Ephesians 1:7 says that redemption is through His blood.

Now let's look at Isaiah 43. It is packed with the proclamation that Jesus Christ has to be God. Listen: Starting in verse 10 we read that God says He is God and was always God and that there is no other god before Him, nor shall there be another god after Him. Then He says this: I, even I, am the LORD; and beside Me there is no Savior (notice the capital LORD). But we know that Jesus Christ says the same thing! Beside Him, Jesus, there is no Savior (Acts 4:12). In Isaiah 43 verses 12 through 15, listen to the names God gives Himself...all in four little verses. He says He is God, Redeemer, the Holy One, Lord, Creator and King. All are names of Christ Jesus.

In Isaiah 43: 25 God says: "I, even I, am He that blots out your transgressions." Well, we know that it is the Lord Jesus who blots out our transgressions with His own blood. "Come now, and let us reason together, says the LORD: though your sins are as scarlet, they shall be as white as snow" (Isaiah 1:18).

Now in Isaiah 45:22 God says something amazing. He says: "Look unto Me and be saved...I am God." Now let's go back to the Israelites in the desert when Moses made a bronze serpent and raised it up on a pole. The serpent on the pole was a foreshadowing of Jesus Christ hanging as sin on the cross. Remember that the people were told simply to look to the serpent on the pole raised up and they would be saved. Well, God is using the same words in this verse in Isaiah and we know that it refers to all sinners looking to Jesus on the cross to be saved. How do we know that? Because Jesus said: "Just as Moses lifted up the serpent in the wilderness, so the Son of man must be lifted up" (John 3:14). Jesus tells us in His own words that He is the same one who told the Israelites in the wilderness to look to Him alone for salvation. Isaiah, speaking for God, says the same thing... "Look to Me and be saved." But look again... "Look to Me and be saved... I am God." What were the Israelites in the wilderness told to look to? They were told to look to the serpent on the pole and be saved. The serpent on the pole represented Jesus, made to be sin (2 Corinthians 5:21), on the cross...God on the cross. He said... "I AM GOD".

Now let's look at Isaiah 45:23. It is undeniable that this scripture is claiming that Jesus and God are the same...they are one. God says: "I have sworn by Myself, the word is gone out of My mouth in righteousness, and shall not return, that unto Me every knee shall bow and every tongue shall swear." This is clearly Jehovah God speaking. God swears by Himself, remember, because there is none greater than He.

Paul says this exact thing in Philippians 2:10-11. Listen: "That at the name of Jesus every knee shall bow and every tongue confess that Jesus Christ is Lord." We have Jehovah God, and Jesus Christ who is God the Son, showing themselves to be the same. They are one God in three persons.

Isaiah says in chapter 47:4, "As for our Redeemer, the LORD of Hosts is His name, the Holy One of Israel." This is Jehovah God who Isaiah is calling Redeemer. Now let's go back to Job 19:25 for a minute. Job is exclaiming in exuberant revelation that he knows his Redeemer lives, and will stand at the Last Day on the earth. Well, this is Jesus who is the Redeemer who will return on the Mount of Olives at the Last Day. Zechariah 14:4 says this: "And His feet shall stand in that day upon the Mount of Olives..." Zechariah is clearly prophesying of the Last Day where it is Jesus Christ who returns at the Second Coming of Christ and His feet part the Mount of Olives. Job calls Him Redeemer and He is referring to Jehovah God.

Now we come to Isaiah 48. Be still, my heart! Listen to this oration from Jesus Christ. Isaiah is speaking in the voice of Jehovah God but at the same time it is Jesus. He identifies over and over again who He is and calls the Trinity each by name, identifying that they are three in one. It is Jehovah talking in the voice of the prophet Isaiah saying that He is the First and the Last, just like Jesus claims of Himself in Revelation. He says that it was His hand that laid out the foundation of the earth. He says that His right hand has stretched out the Heavens. Oh, my, my...then He says this: "Come near to Me, hear this: I have not spoken in secret from the beginning; from the time it was, I was there." Now, look at what Jesus says in John 18:20: He says, "...In secret have I said nothing..." The same wording is intentional. It is God in each case who is saying it. It is the Holy Spirit who is writing it.

"And now the Lord God, and His Spirit have sent Me" (Isaiah 48:16). Hallelujah! Oh praise the glorious King! We have God the Father, God the Spirit and God the Son identified right here. God is one. God is Jesus Christ! Look again: The Lord God, His Spirit and Me. Me means Jesus. Does your heart not just melt right here...you who have not believed yet but will? Look... "I have not spoken in secret..." Can't you hear Him pleading with you, unbeliever? He has put it in plain sight for you. He loves you so much but you must receive Him as God. How can you deny your God? It is your dark and hardened heart that won't see. Just open your dark eyes and you will see. But let's move on.

Isaiah 49 continues this oration from Christ. It is almost as if He is lamenting... "Look at Me! I am your God!"

He says, "The LORD has called Me (Jesus) from the womb; from the matrix of My mother He has made mention of My name (a virgin shall conceive and bring forth a Son and His name shall be called 'Wonderful, Counselor, the Mighty God, the Everlasting Father, the Prince of Peace'). And He has made My mouth like a sharp sword..." We know this is Jesus Christ who conquers with the sword of His mouth. The oration continues claiming that Jesus is glorious in the eyes of the LORD. He is God's Servant to bring back Israel and to be a light to the gentiles. Then He says that He is despised (we know that it is Jesus who is despised yet He despised not) but that kings and princes will arise to worship Him. Why? It is because God has chosen Him (Isaiah 49:7). Isaiah 49: 8 continues and says that Jesus has been given as a covenant to the people to restore the earth. He has come to set free the captives and to bring light to darkness. He will comfort His people and have mercy on them.

Then He says something amazing. He says, "But Zion (Israel) said, The LORD has forsaken me." But God says this: "Can a mother forget her nursing child....I will not forget you." The church has not replaced Israel, and neither will the Jehovah's Witnesses. God has a plan for this flock too. They will also come to faith (as a nation) in the Last Day. He has inscribed them (Israel) on the palms of His hands. How could He forget them? With nails He has done it.

Isaiah 50 speaks of Christ being despised though He came to save. It begins with God the Father speaking of how Israel has turned from Him. Then, the same person says that He is the one who speaks and the waters are dried up (like the Red Sea parting and the Last Day events in Revelation) etc. This is God. This same voice says that He learned obedience from the Father (Hebrews 5:8) and was not rebellious to His call to be slaughtered. Isaiah 50:6 says, "I gave My back to those who struck Me, and my cheeks to those who plucked out My beard; I did not hide My face from shame and spitting."

This is my Christ, my God. This is Jesus who is speaking and notice that He began speaking as Jehovah God. They are one. He says that the LORD God will help Him and therefore He will not be disgraced. He will not be ashamed.

Isaiah 51 speaks of God saying that He will judge the peoples in the day He saves. We know that Jesus judges all men; the saved at the Judgment Seat of Christ and the unsaved at the Great White Throne judgment. Jesus sits as judge at both judgments. But here we see it is Jehovah God who says He sits as judge.

Now we are getting to the most awesome chapter in the Bible, Isaiah 53, where we see the Lamb of God slain; but before that let's look at chapter 52. Look at verse 6; it says something very intriguing. "Behold it is I." This is indisputably God speaking.

Now jump to Matthew 14:27 where Jesus says to the disciples as He is walking on water to their boat, "It is I."

This is also intentional on the part of the Holy Spirit to show that they are one in the same. Isaiah 52:10 says that God has made bare His holy arm. He has made Himself vulnerable in other words as the Christ, the Son of God.

Who Has Believed Our Report?

Chapter 53 opens with these penetrating words: "WHO has believed our report?" This is the Godhead speaking; Father, Son and Holy Spirit (**our** report). "And to whom has the arm of the LORD been revealed?" This is Christ, the arm of the LORD. The question is "To whom has Christ been revealed?" Then Isaiah goes on to give the most gut wrenching account of our Lord's crucifixion.

"He grew up before Him as a tender shoot; as a root out of dry ground." "He was despised and we esteemed Him not." This is God who we did not esteem. This is Christ who was revealed, yet despised. To whom was He revealed? To His own. By whom was He despised? By His own...they esteemed Him not as God. He revealed Himself as God but they esteemed Him not as God. Neither do the Witnesses honor Him as God.

Those who deny that He is God...because He says He is God... despise Him still. "Our chastisement was upon Him, but by HIS wounds WE are healed." Christ Jesus paid for sin that was not His (2 Corinthians 5:21).

The Jehovah's Witnesses try to atone for their own sin but they cannot do it. If they remain what they are when they die they will find themselves standing before a holy and perfect God who will demand payment for their sin and they will have nothing with which to pay it because they never let Christ pay their debt. He is the only one who can do it and He freely gives life and freedom from the bondage of sin yet they are arrogant enough to think they can foot the bill by their good works.

Now look in chapter 54. God is telling us that the shame of our youth we will forget because we are washed in His blood. He says this: "For your Maker is your Husband. The LORD of Hosts is His name..." This is Jesus Christ who is the Bridegroom, the Husband of the church.

Look at Isaiah 62:11. Isaiah says, "Surely your salvation is coming; Behold, His reward is with Him." This is Jehovah God spoken of here. Well, let's skip to Revelation 22:12 where we read this: "Behold, I am coming quickly and My reward is with Me." This is Jesus Christ saying the same thing Jehovah God said in Isaiah.

In chapter 63 we read about God Almighty coming in judgment (because we know it is only God who judges) in the Last Day. Isaiah 63:1 asks us who it is that is coming to the earth with blood stained garments. The answer, we know, is that this is Jesus Christ. But Isaiah is showing us that it is Jehovah God.

Isaiah 63:2 (NJKV) says, "Why is Your apparel red and Your garments like one who treads the winepress?" But we know this is Jesus Christ who comes in wrath and judgment in Revelation where we see that His robe is stained with blood because of His wrath against the unbelievers. Isaiah 63:3 says that He has trodden the winepress alone in His anger and trampled them in His fury. He said that he has stained His robes with THEIR (those who have rejected Christ) blood this time. Isaiah 63:4 says that vengeance is in His (God's) heart. Paul quotes Isaiah in Romans 12:19 and tells us it is the **Lord** who said it...but Isaiah tells us in the context he is saying it that the **LORD** Jehovah God said it! They are the same.

"He that has seen Me, has seen the Father" (John 14:9).

We see this same idea in chapter 61 where Isaiah is prophesying concerning the acceptable year of the LORD.

Jesus quotes this scripture and leaves off the part of the day of vengeance mentioned in Isaiah 61:2. He did this because at the time He spoke it He was presenting Himself in a different role than He will in the Last Day. He is first Lamb, then Lion.

Now I mention these vengeance scriptures to show that Jesus was not just God's instrument for carrying out that vengeance, which He will in the Last Day, but to show that vengeance belongs to the LORD. Vengeance belongs to God, but Jesus says that this is His vengeance...clearly showing us that Jesus is God. Psalm 94:1 says that vengeance belongs to God.

Also, look at Isaiah 63:5. After Jehovah God tells us that vengeance is in His heart in the Last Day (verse 4), He goes on to ponder something. He says in verse 5 that He looked around Himself and noticed that there was no one to help Him...He was alone (God is the one who is alone with Himself here). Then He says that His own arm will bring salvation and His fury will uphold Him. Remember that the arm of the LORD is Jesus Christ. This is Jesus and Jehovah calling the arm of the LORD His and His alone...they are the same.

Isaiah 63:10 says that His wayward children rebelled against His Spirit and grieved His Holy Spirit, so He (the Holy Spirit) turned against them and fought against them. So who fought against them? The Holy Spirit did.

In Isaiah 64 the prophet Isaiah is speaking to Jehovah God and says with longing, "Oh that You would rend the heavens, that You would come down!" And then Isaiah longs for the mountains to flow down at His presence and for the nations to tremble at His presence. We know this is Jehovah God Isaiah is speaking of and to. Well, this is just a description of what Jesus Christ will do at His Second Coming. He will return to earth in wrath on the Mount of Olives and it will part. Revelation 16:20 tells us that the mountains will disappear at Christ's coming and verse 19 says that the cities of the nations will fall.

Now, let's look at something very interesting in Ezekiel. Look at chapter 36, verse 23: Ezekiel records God's words as He says... "And the heathen shall know that I am the LORD, says the Lord God..." Jehovah's Witnesses have argued in my living room that when we see LORD in all capital letters that this is Jehovah God but when we see Lord written with only the "L" capitalized, that this is just a title of a dignitary. They may argue that the Lord used here is just a title God is using of Himself but any reasonable mind can see otherwise. We know of course that dignitaries are called Lord sometimes, but here we see again that Jehovah God is referring to Himself using both ways of writing the name LORD. Jehovah's Witnesses will claim that Jesus is not referred to as God when He is given the title Lord...small letters. This verse proves them wrong. Besides, isn't it true that when a dignitary is being referenced, all small case letters are used? I am not sure about that and don't feel compelled to look it up because it is irrelevant to what I am saying. The truth is that LORD and Lord are used interchangeably when referencing Jehovah God and Jesus Christ...both are the one true God.

In Daniel we come to another very interesting appearance of the pre-incarnate Christ. Look at Shadrach, Meshach and Abednego as they are thrown into the fiery furnace: There is a fourth "man" walking around with them in the furnace. Nebuchadnezzar says that it looks like the Son of God! He was right! It was the Son of God even before He came in the flesh. Jesus Christ always was, always is and always will be. He created all things and has always been, because Jesus Christ is Jehovah.

In Daniel chapter 10, Daniel is giving an account of the vision he was given by God of Christ as we see Him in Revelation. His face is like lightening and His eyes are fire...this is Christ as He will appear when He returns to earth in wrath to destroy the wicked.

Hosea is a wonderful book that illustrates God's judgment towards Israel because of her unfaithfulness, and His sweet undying mercy towards His people. The end of the book tells us clearly that God has not forgotten and will not forget Israel, but that there is coming a day when she will be completely restored to Him. This happens during the Great Tribulation where the 144,000 Jews are filled with the knowledge of God and receive Christ Jesus as their Messiah at last. God is not finished with Israel and the church is not spiritual Israel and the Jehovah's Witnesses are not the 144,000 Jews of Revelation.

The prophet Amos tells us in chapter nine that God will utterly destroy Israel, but not completely. He will sift her severely but there will remain a faithful remnant. He says in verse 15 that He will plant them again in their land and they will prosper and they will not be pulled out of their land ever again! This will happen sooner than we think. They have already in this generation been restored to their land as a nation, and no matter what we hear on the news today, God tells us that they will not be pulled out of their land ever again. I believe we are not far from this 70th week of Daniel where all Israel will be restored to God through Christ Jesus.

Now look at Micah: We see the Last Day events that Christ performs prophesied of again. Micah says it is the LORD (Jehovah God) who comes down from His Holy temple and causes the mountains to melt at His treading on them and they also part.

This is prophesied again in Revelation and tells of the events in the Last Day when Christ returns and makes the mountains split and melt. Remember how prophecy is often written throughout the Bible. It has a current application to

Israel, a hidden application to the church, and then breaks into Last Day events.

Again, look at Nahum 1:5. The prophet says that the mountains quake at His presence and the hills melt and the earth is burned. This has never happened. This is the Last Day spoken of here and again it is Jesus Christ who does this... Nahum says it is God who does it. The prophet Habakkuk also sees in a vision the LORD God coming to earth scattering mountains and making hills bow low. Zephaniah in chapter 3 also mentions that the LORD in His anger will come down in the Last Day and will pour out His anger on the earth with the fire of His jealousy.

Zephaniah ends his prophecy with the sweet mercy of God who restores His beloved Israel.

Zechariah 11:10-13 is the prophecy concerning Jesus being crucified as Messiah and Judas Iscariot who betrays Him for 30 pieces of silver. Look at what Jehovah God says in verse 13: He says with sorrowful sarcasm that Judas should cast that "goodly" price of 30 pieces of silver, at which he valued Christ, to the potter...which he did, and hanged himself there. The words are: "A goodly price that I was prized at of them." In other words...God is saying: "This is what I am worth to them; thirty pieces of silver." We know it is the LORD who is speaking and saying that He Himself was prized at this price. We also know that Judas betrayed Jesus for this same price. Jesus is God.

Oh my, it just gets better and better. Now as we get to Zechariah 12, let's look at verses 8-10. Jehovah God is talking and He is telling Zechariah what will happen in the Last Day. He starts by saying that He, the LORD, will defend the inhabitants of Jerusalem; that He, the LORD, will destroy the nations that come against Jerusalem; and that He will pour out upon Jerusalem, the spirit of grace and supplications. Then He says, and it is still Jehovah God talking: "They shall look upon Me, whom they have pierced, and shall mourn over Him, as one that is in bitterness for his firstborn." The 144,000 Jews who will be saved by coming to the knowledge of Christ during the Great Tribulation period are those who will mourn when they see who it is that they not only crucified but rejected as their Messiah. They will see who Jesus Christ really is and will receive Him with mourning and remorse. This is one of the most fascinating verses in the Bible to me. I pray that those who have denied that Christ is God will see what is hidden here in plain sight.

Now we see in Zechariah 13:5 that Zechariah is talking about the Second Coming of Christ. He mentions in verse 4 that Jesus will stand on the Mount of Olives and it will split. Verse 5 says: "The LORD my God shall come, and all the saints with Him." Here we are told that it is the LORD God who returns with His saints, but Revelation tells us that it is Christ Jesus who returns with His saints…and these saints are the raptured believers who have been with Him in Heaven while the wrath of God is poured out upon the earth.

The Old Testament is in the New Testament Concealed; The New Testament is in the Old Testament Revealed

Now here we are at the New Testament. Please notice that everything we have covered so far has included intermittently both the Old and New Testaments. They are so tightly woven together that they cannot be separated. As someone so cleverly stated… "The Old Testament is in the New Testament concealed and the New Testament is in the Old Testament revealed." That is important to point out. Truth is discovered by knowing the entire Word of God and not just part of it.

Almost as soon as Matthew opens, we read in chapter 2 that Herod tries to find where the Christ child is so he could worship Him. Of course he was lying, we're told, because Herod really wanted to kill Christ. But he knew that this Christ was to be worshiped and only God is worshiped.

Now in Matthew 2:11 we see something even more amazing: The wise men, when they found Christ, fell down and worshiped Him. If you are tempted to say that they were wrong in doing that, look at verse 12: It says that God warned them in a dream not to go back to Herod but to go to their own country by another way. Their worship was received. They were not chastened for worshiping this Christ child but were blessed by receiving further revelation.

In Matthew 9:18 we see that a certain ruler came to Jesus and worshiped Him...Jesus does not stop him. Now either Jesus allows the man to worship Him because Jesus is God or he has just done something blasphemous. Anyone can see here that we have to conclude by this passage alone that either Jesus is God or He isn't even worthy of any honor.

Look, in Matthew 10:33 Jesus says that any man who denies Him before men, He will deny before the Father. The Jehovah's Witnesses deny Christ because they deny that He is God in the flesh. In fact, they go door to door specifically to enter unsuspecting homes just so they can deny Christ before men. But this is Jesus' own claim of Himself. They deny the gospel Christ taught of Himself and therefore will be denied before God. He will say that He never knew them, because He will not have.

In Matthew 15:25 we see that the woman with an issue of blood also worshiped Jesus; He didn't stop her as all other angels do and say, "Get up, I am just a messenger, or servant." Instead He received her worship and declared that she had great faith.

Alright, here in chapter 19:16-17 we see someone come up to Jesus and call Him "Good Master", but Jesus responds to this person by asking him why it is that he calls Him "good"?

Then Jesus says, "For none is good except the Father." I really believe that Jesus is claiming to be God in this verse. It is as if He is saying, "You say I am good, but none is good except Jehovah God so I must be Him." Notice that Jesus doesn't say that He is not good but He just makes the person think about what caused him to call Him "good"... very interesting.

In Matthew 20, we see James' and John's mother worshiping Jesus and He receives it again. At the end of Matthew 22, we see Jesus asking the Pharisees whose son the Christ is. They say that Christ is the son of David, but Jesus stumps them when He says, "How can Christ be David's son when David calls the Christ, 'Lord'"? They have no answer. I think the Jehovah's Witnesses are a lot like the Pharisees. They, as a whole, don't want to believe.

Now look at Matthew 23:34. Jesus is speaking woes to the Pharisees. He says in verse 34, "Behold, I send unto you prophets and wise men and scribes..." Who sent prophets and wise men to the world? Jehovah God alone did! Why then does Jesus say that HE sent them and will continue to send them? The unavoidable answer is that Jesus is Jehovah God in the form of the Son, God the Son. Father and Son are one, they are God.

In chapter 26 we see that Jesus is accused by the Pharisees of blasphemy and this is the reason they say they want to crucify Him (even though later we are told that they were envious of Him). Well, what did He say that would cause them to bring this claim against Christ? They knew that Jesus was not claiming just to be the Son of God, but He said that He was God; over and over again He said it.

Here in Matthew 27, after our Lord's arrest, we see the prophecy of the thirty pieces of silver fulfilled. Remember that it was God speaking through Zechariah when this prophecy was given and it was God who said of Himself, "They valued Me so little as to put a price of thirty pieces of silver on Me."

Matthew ends with the record of His resurrection appearance to the eleven disciples. Matthew says when they saw Him they worshiped Him. He received this worship. Then the book ends with Jesus' admonition to the disciples to go and tell all nations and baptize in the name of the Father, the Son and the Holy Ghost. Jesus did not say "baptize in the NAMES of them but the name...they are one. This is a clear reference to the Trinity.

In Mark chapter 1 we see the book open with the Trinity. At the baptism of Christ we see the Son, the Father and the Holy Spirit present for this occasion. In verse 24 we see that the demons know who He is..."the Holy One of God".

We continue to see that all are amazed at Christ's authority to cast out demons and to heal and to forgive sins...no one but God can do that and this was well understood. This is the reason for their astonishment. "What kind of doctrine is this?" they said.

In Luke 2:11 we see that an angel announces the birth of Christ and calls Him Christ the Lord, our Savior. Now skip to chapter 7 and let's look at the story of John the Baptist. Notice that Jesus treats John the Baptist in a similar way that Jehovah God treated Job. God was to Job what may seem harsh to some. But, speaking to Satan at the beginning of the book, God praises Job to the extreme. God declares that Job is perfect and upright; that there is no one like him on earth. Jesus does the same thing here concerning John the Baptist.

John was confused because he thought Jesus would be King right then. He did not understand about the Second Coming of Christ. He sent a message to Jesus asking Him if He was the one they had been expecting. Jesus doesn't answer directly or even try to console John. He never even visits him in prison. He simply sends word that the blind see and the lame walk, etc. Then Jesus does something curious. He praises John to the extreme before the people who were gathered before Him. Remember that Jesus says that of all men born of woman, none is greater than John. How mysterious is our God? God was not interested in coddling Job and neither was Jesus interested in coddling John. But both the Father and the Son behaved in the exact same way. This is because they both are God in two different persons of the Trinity and they both have the omniscience to know that consoling would come later for both men and that their rewards, which will be so great, would be more than enough to erase any pain they may have suffered for His sake. What wisdom!

We see in Luke 8:39 that Jesus says to a man out of whom He had just cast many devils: "Return unto thy house and show how great things God has done unto thee." Then the next verse says: "Then he went and told the great things Jesus had done unto him." First, Jesus said God had done this to him and then Luke says that Jesus had done this to him. The Holy Spirit is showing those who have eyes to see that Jesus is God. The mentioning of both persons of the Godhead as doing the same thing is intentional. It is the Holy Spirit who is God, who is showing us that Jesus is God.

We see this happen again in Luke. In Luke 12:12, Jesus is instructing the disciples how to respond to persecution that will come to them as they follow Christ and teach the gospel of Christ. He says that when they are brought to the synagogues, magistrates and powers that they should take no thought of how they should answer or what they should say. He says that the **Holy Spirit** will teach them in the same hour what they should say. Now let's skip to Luke 21:14-15. Jesus says the same thing. Only this time He tells them that **He** will give them a mouth and wisdom. In other words, it is now Jesus who will give them in the same hour what they are to say. Here it is: "…they shall deliver you up to the synagogues, before kings and rulers. Settle it therefore in your hearts, not to meditate beforehand what to answer: For I will give you a mouth and wisdom..." (Luke 21:12-15). First of all, this is also intentional that the two statements are speaking of the same event but using each time a different person of the Trinity. Again, Jesus in chapter 12 tells the disciples that He is forewarning them of a time in the future when they will be brought up before the synagogues, magistrates and powers. He says they should not think of what they should say because the **Holy Spirit** will give them what they are to say. In Luke 21, Jesus is reiterating what He already warned them of beforehand...only in the first case He says the **Holy Spirit** will give them what to say and in the second case He says that **He** will give them what to say. This is because Jesus is God. This is God the Holy Spirit spoken of first and then God the Son spoken of next...they are one in the same. Just look at the assurance that this is the same event Jesus is just restating. In the first case we see the synagogues, the magistrates and powers. In the second case we see the synagogues, kings and rulers.

The last chapter in Luke records the ascension of Jesus as the disciples watched. We read that they worshiped Him. Now, for argument's sake, if someone wants to claim that they did not know any better then just look at Luke 24:45. We see that Jesus had just opened their eyes to the scriptures. They had been given revelation of the truth. They knew who they were worshiping.

The gospel of John has the most blatant and irrefutable evidence that Christ Jesus is God; John opens his gospel by saying it in as many ways as he can and then restating it. But look at John 2:19-21. Jesus tells the Jews that the temple will be destroyed, but in three days He will raise it again. Jesus was referring to the temple of His body being crucified and that in three days He would rise, but look who He says will raise His body. Jesus said that HE would raise it! Hallelujah.

We will see later in the Word that it is the Holy Spirit who raises His body! Father, Son and the Holy Spirit are One!

Not only was it He who laid it down (no man took it from Him) but it would be Jesus who would raise His own body from the dead, and He would do it as the person of the Holy Spirit! Oh Lord God, Your ways are beyond finding out...just as You have said. Praise You!

If We Know the Father, Then We Will Also Know the Son

Now here is a stern warning to those who will not hear the Words of Christ concerning Himself. In John 5:19-24 we hear Jesus explaining His role as the Son. He says that all judgment has been given to Him by the Father, that He does nothing unless the Father tells Him to. This does not tell us that Jesus is not God, but Jesus is explaining His submissive role as the Son of God. Then He warns that anyone who will receive His testimony of Himself has everlasting life. But anyone who does not receive this testimony does not know the Son and therefore does not know the Father...even though they think they do.

I am afraid that the Jehovah's Witnesses prove they don't even know Jehovah God because they deny what Christ says concerning Himself. These are the Lord's own words. This is a very frightening warning to those who have denied Christ is who He says He is.

In John 5:39-40 we see Christ continuing to warn the Jews who refused to believe Christ's testimony of Himself. He says that they think they have eternal life in the scriptures but that these very scriptures they claim to love and follow only testify of Christ. He said that they proved that the Word of God (which they appeared to love but didn't) was not in them because they rejected Christ, whereby rejecting all that the Word claims. In verse 40 Christ says: "And you will not come to Me that you may have life." This is so sad. Neither will the Jehovah's Witnesses as long as they are such ever come to Christ for life. They believe they have life by being good. But Jesus said that only God is good, and to have life, we must come to Him and partake of His life.

Jesus says in John 6:44 that no man can come to Him unless the Father draws him. So my prayer for those who have been caught in the Witnesses' snare is that the Father will draw them, by His Spirit into the truth of Christ.

Now let's look at John 8:24. Jesus is telling the Jews who were accusing Him that they would die in their sins because they would not believe that, in Christ's own words: "I am." He is using one of many "I am" statements. The King James translation reads "I am He." But the word "He" is added for emphasis. It is not there in the original texts. Jesus is saying that because the Jews would not believe that He is "I am", that they would die in their sins. The same goes for anyone, including the Witnesses, who refuses to believe that Jesus is God, the Great I AM.

In John 8:58 Jesus is continuing to tell the Jews that if they knew the Father then they would know Him, but they don't know Him therefore they do not know the Father. He said that even Abraham, whom they say is their father, saw Jesus' day and was glad. The Jews get angry here because Jesus says in essence, "How can you be children of Abraham when you don't see what he saw and rejoiced in." Then comes the ultimate kicker: The Jews fire back at Jesus by saying to Him sarcastically that He (Jesus) is not even 50 years old so how can He claim to have seen Abraham.

Jesus responds with something that knocked them for a loop…so much so that they wanted to kill Him even more at this point because of what He was claiming by the following statement. Jesus simply responded by saying, "Before Abraham was, I am." Jesus is again calling Himself the Great

Whose Witnesses?

I AM, and they knew it! They understood perfectly that Jesus was telling them that He is God (Missler's commentaries).

Oh, this gospel by John is just full of powerful truth. Look at the next event in chapter 9. Jesus heals the blind man; who was blind we are told in order that he might be healed and glorify God. The Pharisees inquire of the man's parents first and then the man himself. They want to know who this man is that healed him. He says that he does not know, but one thing he does know is that he was blind and now he can see. This infuriates the Pharisees and this simple man says something so profound that it sends them into orbit with anger. They ask the formerly blind man what Jesus did to him to heal him. The man replies that he already told them but they did not hear.

Then the man says: "Why do you want to know…so you can also be His disciples?" They reviled him because of his sarcasm and reply that they are Moses' disciples. They say that they know that God spoke to Moses but as for this man (Jesus) they don't know where He comes from. The man replies with a piercing truth. He says, "This is a marvelous thing that you don't know where He comes from and yet He has opened my eyes."

This is a stinging truth spoken by a seemingly foolish and simple man. He marvels at how it was even possible that such wise men claiming to know God could be so blind and yet he, a simple man, who had been blind, could see the truth. Jesus said to the Father, remember, "I thank You Father that You have hid this from the wise and revealed it to the babes." It is the same prideful "wisdom" that blinds the Jehovah's Witnesses from seeing the simple truth of Christ today.

This story ends when Jesus finds this man again after the Pharisees had cast him out and asks the man if he believes on the Son of God. The man so sweetly and simply answers by asking Jesus who the Son of God is and Jesus says "You have both seen Him and it is He who talks to you." The man instantly believes and WORSHIPS Christ as God. There is no investigation or pondering on his part...he just believes!

Now look at this: In John 10:33, the Jews want to stone Jesus because He said He was God! **Jesus Christ said He was God**...the Jews say it right here. This is why they want to stone Him. How in the world can a Jehovah's Witness say anything good about Jesus then? They claim that He is absolutely not God (just like the Pharisees whom Jesus said would die in their sins because they didn't believe Jesus was who He said He was). Jesus said He was God. They would have to label Him a blasphemer as well. They think they see but are blind and dead in their sins if they do not come to believe that Jesus is who He said He is...Jehovah God.

I want to add something here. If a Jehovah's Witness knocks on your door and you don't want to engage them then do this one thing and it will work every time: Tell them that Jesus Christ is Jehovah God and they will turn and leave...I promise. Try it and see. This is because the truth of His Godhead silences them. And it is this one truth that they are vehemently opposed to. The foundation of their false doctrine is to deny that Jesus is God...all else is secondary.

Look at something amazing in John 12:37-41. This is an incredible portion of scripture. Not only is the Holy Spirit taking one more opportunity to show that Jesus is Almighty God but He is also reminding the reader that the prophet Isaiah was talking about any group or person who believes another gospel (like the Jehovah's Witnesses) and how they will be blinded and not healed because of their darkened hearts that refused to hear the truth.

John records in this instance that the Pharisees are just fulfilling what the prophet Isaiah said about them. He said that they would have darkened eyes (understanding) because their hearts were dark. Then John says this: "Isaiah said this because he saw Jesus' glory and spoke about Him" (John

12:41). Whose glory did Isaiah see? Well, here John says Isaiah saw Jesus' glory. But we know from Isaiah 6:1-3 that Isaiah saw the glory of Jehovah God. So we know once again that the Holy Spirit is showing us that Jehovah God and Jesus Christ are both Almighty God; they are the Father and the Son of the Trinity.

Now if that is not enough, look again at what the Holy Spirit does for us: In Isaiah 6:1 Isaiah says he is looking at the glory of God "high and lifted up". Let's go back to John 12:30-34 which is the section of scripture that is just before John's statement that Isaiah saw the glory of Jesus. In it Jesus is saying that He must be lifted up from the earth to draw all men unto Himself. The Holy Spirit did this for our benefit. This portion of scripture so strongly proves that the Almighty who is high and lifted up is also Jesus Christ who was high and lifted up. Like Isaiah said in the same scripture, we have to be blind not to see it.

God says that He will make sure that a dark heart that refuses the true gospel will remain dark so that it will not be healed. This is so clear to the heart that desires only God. Let's look at Roman's 1:20-21. Paul says that God has made Himself known to all. Man is without excuse for not knowing God. He says those who deny Him will be given over to a debased mind that cannot know Him. This is because although they knew God, they did not glorify Him as God. This is just like the Pharisees who said that they knew God, and Jesus said that they didn't because if they did then they would have known who Jesus was also. They proved that because they knew not who Christ was that they also did not know Jehovah God. This is what the Jehovah's Witnesses do.

Jesus consoles the disciples in John 14 as He tells them that He is about to return to Heaven. He tells them that they know the way. This is where Jesus makes the well-known statement "I am the way the truth and the life and no man can come to the Father but by Me". Then in verse 7 Jesus tells them that now they DO know the Father and have seen Him. In John 14:9, Jesus tells Philip that if he has seen Jesus then he has also seen the Father. Jesus goes on to say that He is in the Father and the Father is in Him...they are one. Jesus warns in verses 23 & 24 that the one who loves Him will keep His words and the one who doesn't love Him will not keep His words. We are not keeping His Word if we deny it.

In John 14:8 & 9 we see Philip asking Jesus to show them the Father. Jesus responds by saying to Philip: "Have I been with you this long and still you don't know Me?" Philip had asked to see the Father. Jesus said in essence... "Here I am!"

Now in John 14:26 we see that Jesus says the Comforter who is the Holy Spirit will come to them and teach them all things and bring to remembrance what Jesus has said to them. In John 18:5 & 8 we see Jesus calling Himself "I am" again. The word *he* does not belong there. It is not in the earliest transcripts but was added to the English translation for clarity. He is claiming to be the Great "I AM".

In John 20:28 we see that Thomas doubted that Jesus had been raised from the dead and said that he would never believe until he saw Him with his own eyes and touched His wounds. Jesus appears to him then and tells Thomas to look at Him and thrust his hands into His side. Thomas exclaims: "My Lord and my God!" Thomas was calling Jesus God and Jesus does not correct him.

Now in Acts 2:32 and numerous places elsewhere we see that God raised Jesus up after the crucifixion. So far, we have been told in the Word that Jesus raised Himself up, then the Holy Spirit raised Him up and now it is Jehovah God who raised Him up. Again, this is for eyes that want to see and ears that want to hear. All three persons of the Godhead raised Christ up.

Acts 2 closes as Peter is explaining to the Jews with simplicity that Christ is Lord. They receive the truth upon hearing it (as a matter of fact, they were pricked in the heart) and immediately ask Peter what they must do. Peter simply says what I would repeat right now to anyone who has not received Christ Jesus as Lord; that is, as God. Peter says: "Repent and be baptized in the name of Jesus Christ for the remission of sins, and you shall receive the gift of the Holy Ghost."

Because the Jehovah's Witnesses deny that the Holy Spirit is a person, I have mentioned a few verses that show Him as a person. Acts 8:28 is a good one that does just that. Look: Philip (another Philip, it seems) runs into a eunuch who is studying the Word as he rides along in his chariot and is wondering what it all meant. We read that "The Spirit said to Philip, 'Go near...'". The Holy Spirit **said.** The Holy Spirit is a person.

Now we read in Colossians 1:15-17 that Jesus is the image of the invisible God. By Him (Jesus) were all things created in heaven and earth, both visible and invisible...all things were created by Him and for Him. He is before all things and by Him all things consist. This can't be manipulated. Jesus is declared here by Paul to be the Creator of the Universe.

In Colossians 3:24 we see Paul admonishing the church to do whatever work God has given us knowing in our hearts that it is Christ the Lord we are serving. If Christ is not God, then this admonition by Paul would be encouraging the church into idolatry. We live to serve God and not a celestial being.

Paul ends the first letter to Timothy by declaring that God is the only Ruler, that He is the King of Kings and the Lord of lords, who alone is immortal and dwells in unapproachable light. I could end this book here because what else needs to be said? Paul says that God is the King of kings and the Lord of lords...but this is Jesus' title in Revelation 17 & 19. Paul says that God alone is immortal but Jesus says in Revelation that He is the one who lives forever…immortal.

God Our Savior

Paul in his letter to Titus calls God "our Savior" in chapter 1 Verse 3. In Titus 1:4 Paul says that Christ Jesus is our Savior. Then in Titus 2:13, we read that Paul says: "…looking for that blessed hope, and the glorious appearing of the great God and our Savior Jesus Christ." The King James Version has the word "and" there but others do not. The right understanding of this verse is that Paul is calling Jesus both Christ and God. So the actual wording is this: "…looking for the glorious appearing of the great God our Savior Jesus Christ." It is a shame that the KJV added the word "and".

The writer of Hebrews opens the book by declaring that God created the universe through Christ. He goes on to say that Christ is the radiance of God's glory, that He is the exact representation of His being, sustaining all things by His powerful Word.

This is God's Word but here we see that it is Christ's Word…remember it is so much Christ's Word (the Word of God) that John says He **IS** the Word made flesh. Then we see in Hebrews 1:4 that Christ became as much higher than the angels as His name is higher than theirs. What? We see in Hebrews 2:7 & 9 that Jesus was made a little lower than the angels. This sounds like a contradiction but it isn't. This is a wonderful example of how Jesus Christ is both God and man. As man, the Son of God, He held a position that was a little lower than the angels. This, as explained in verse 9, was so that He could taste death for every man. God had to become a man to pay for the sins of man. But after He stepped back into His pre-incarnate glory as God Almighty, He became once again as high above the angels as His name is above their name. And remember that His name is "Wonderful",

"Counselor", "The Mighty God", "The Everlasting Father", "The Prince of Peace".

If Christ is an archangel like the Witness' doctrine claims, then why does the writer of Hebrews specifically contradict that claim? Hebrews 1:5 says: "For which of the angels did God ever say, 'You are My Son, today, I have become Your Father'"? Then Hebrews 1:6 says: "And again, when God brings His firstborn into the world, He says, 'Let all the angels worship Him'".

Then…look what Almighty God says to Jesus Christ His Son: Hebrews 1:8 says: "But to the Son He (God) says, 'Your throne, O God, will last forever, and righteousness will be the scepter of Your kingdom…'" Almighty, Jehovah God is calling Jesus the Son, "God". Jehovah God says that Jesus Christ is God. Wow! This should be all we need to know.

Jesus is called God by God. We don't have to understand it to believe it. We know for example that God has no beginning or end. We believe it because He said it. I can't comprehend that with my tiny brain, can you? It is incomprehensible to our limited minds. So is the fact that God is one God yet in three persons. Faith is always a matter of the heart and we have to always keep in the forefront of our minds that His ways are beyond finding out.

Now let's look at 1 John 5:7. This is an incredibly clear verse which tells us that God is three in one. John says: **"For there are three that bear record in Heaven, the Father, the Word and the Holy Ghost: and these three are one."** We already know that the Word is Jesus Christ. John clearly tells us that God is Father, Son and Holy Spirit…He is three but one. Thank You God for such clarity and simplicity.

In the tiny book of Jude we read at the closing of it that Jude dedicates the book to "The only wise God, our Savior" (Jude 25). Jesus Christ is our only Savior and He is God.

Now we have come to the last book of the Word of God… the book of Revelation. There is so much here. To start off, just look at what Christ says of Himself right at the outset. He says in Revelation 1:8: "I am the Alpha and the Omega, the beginning and the ending, says the Lord, which is and which was, and which is to come, the Almighty". How can anyone with a sensible mind argue and distort this simple but overwhelming truth? This is Jesus talking. He says He is the one who has always been and the one who will always be. He says He is the Almighty. Jehovah God is the Almighty. Just read it and receive it...don't try to understand it.

Revelation 1:15 says that Jesus' voice as He was speaking to John was like the voice of many waters. But Ezekiel tells us in Ezekiel 43:2 that Jehovah God's voice is like the voice of many waters. Revelation 1:18 tells us that Jesus was alive, then dead and alive again and that He is the one who has the keys of Hell and death. But who is the one we are told who has the ability to throw the soul into Hell? It is Jehovah God. Luke 12:5 says that it is God Almighty who is to be feared because He is the one who can throw body and soul into Hell.

In Revelation 2:7 Jesus is saying: "Hear what the Spirit says..." Then He speaks. He and the Holy Spirit are one... they are God. In Revelation 2:9 the Lord Jesus is saying that some in the Last Days will call themselves Jews but are not and that they are actually a synagogue of Satan. Don't the Witnesses claim they are Jews in essence by claiming they are the 144,000 spoken of in Revelation? Yes they do. We can clearly see that the 144,000 will be comprised of the 12 tribes of Israel and there will be 12,000 from each tribe. Twelve tribes multiplied by 12 thousand people equals 144,000. The Word clearly tells us that this is Israel yet the Witnesses claim they are the 144,000. They are therefore claiming they are the Jews. I believe they are in the group Jesus is speaking of here and Jesus says they are guilty of blasphemy and belong to Satan and his synagogue.

In Revelation 2:23 we see that Jesus says it is He who searches the heart. But we know that only God can look into the heart and that it is He who searches the heart. "Search me oh God and know my heart, try me and know my thoughts, and see if there is any wicked way in me and lead me in the way everlasting" (Psalm 139:23-24).

Now here is a stark warning to Witnesses who persist in their denial of who Christ is. Jesus says in Revelation 3: 8 & 9 that those who keep His Word and don't deny His name will be favored and rewarded greatly. The Witnesses deny Jesus Christ; they deny His name and His gospel and His Word. **He doesn't even warn this group that claims to be Jews but are not to repent...it seems that He just condemns them.**

That is frighteningly serious. I beg those reading this who have denied what the Word says of Christ, to repent now and receive Jesus Christ as Savior and God before it is too late. He is coming soon.

Now we see in Revelation 4 but also in chapters 1 and 3 that the seven Spirits of God are mentioned. This is a detailed study into the Mind of Christ so I won't get into it more here than to say that this is a reference to the Holy Spirit who has seven functions (best word I could find). He is one Spirit with seven functions or attributes that make up the Mind of Christ. These seven functions or attributes are mentioned in Isaiah 11 and can be studied separately. I mention this to show that this reference is also to God...God, the Holy Spirit.

Now in Revelation 4 we see in verse 10 that the elders fall down and worship Him who sits on the throne. We know that it is Jesus who sits on the throne with His Father (chapter 3:21, "with My Father IN His throne"). They are worshiped here and the one seated on the throne is the one who lives forever and ever. This is God. Jesus also says He lives forever and ever...we discussed that earlier. So Jesus is sitting IN the throne of the Father; not beside but IN; and all are worshiping the one who is seated on the throne. Revelation 4:11 records the elders worshiping God on His throne and exclaiming that it is He who has created all things and He is the one for whom all things exist. But we know that Jesus and the Holy Spirit have created all things. The Trinity sits on the throne. Our God is three yet one.

Look at these two verses with me: Revelation 4:11 says: "You are worthy, oh Lord, (notice it is Lord and not LORD) to receive glory and honor and power: for You have created all things, and for Your pleasure they are and were created."

Now look at Colossians 1:16 & 17: "For by Him were all things created...all things were created by Him and for Him: and He is before all things and by Him all things consist." This is Jesus who is spoken of here.

Wow! Now hear this: Revelation 5 says that the Lamb slain before the foundation of the world (Jesus Christ) is the one who has seven horns (all power; omnipotence) seven eyes (eyes meaning Mind of God which is all-knowing; omniscient) and that the seven eyes (Mind of God or Mind of Christ) are also the same thing as the seven Spirits of God. The seven Spirits of God are the Holy Spirit, but also the Mind of Christ! Can we see how tightly interwoven and inseparable they are?

How good of God to reveal this to us. Revelation 5 ends with a picture in Heaven of the elders worshiping God and the Lamb, ascribing to them blessing and honor and glory and power forever.

We see in Revelation 6:10 that the saints who had been beheaded for their faith during the Great Tribulation period, that is yet to come but John was seeing it in advance, were pleading with the Lord (notice the small 'Lord' which is referring to God the Son) to speedily judge and avenge their blood. Who avenges? Jehovah God has said that "Vengeance is Mine says the LORD!" (Romans 12:19). It is Jehovah God who avenges innocent blood, yet here we see Jesus Christ as the Avenger of Blood. Jesus is God. Revelation 6:16 & 17 speaks of the wrath of the Lamb and that no one can stand in this wrath. There is no distinction between the wrath of the Lamb and the wrath of God because they are the same thing...the same event originating from the same person; that is God.

Chapter 7 shows us that God is being worshiped on His throne. We understand that the Lamb is also in the midst of the throne (verse 17) but there is a sense that there is no separateness here between God and the Lamb. We just understand from the reading that there is a throne, THE throne, and God and the Lamb are seated thereon! Those worshiping at the scene have no trouble understanding this and neither should we if we belong to Him.

Now let's look at something very interesting that occurs in many places in the Word but finally here in Revelation. Revelation 7 and 14 tell us that during the Great Tribulation, the faithful will receive a name on their foreheads. Isaiah and Ezekiel also speak of this new name. This name is God's name. Revelation 14:1 says that the 144,000 Jews who have now come to receive Jesus as Messiah at last have been sealed with the name of their God on their foreheads. Well, back in Revelation 3:12 we read in the same verse that this same name is written on the foreheads of them that overcome (faithful believers). In the first part of Revelation 12 Jesus says: "the name of My God", then in the last sentence of verse 12 Jesus says: "I will write upon him My new name." This is the same name and Jesus says it is God's name and it is His name. So which is it? Is it Jehovah's name written on our foreheads or is it Jesus Christ's new name? I will say that it is the same because they are the same person...they are God, Jehovah God. There is much more to this name and receiving our new name...they are connected but this is another topic for another time and it is very delightful!

But for now all I want to point out is that Jesus uses them interchangeably! The identity of the beheaded saints is also a topic for deep study that I won't get into here.

We see in Revelation 12 that the woman clothed with the sun and the moon under her feet and with a crown of twelve stars is a reference to Israel. We can go back to Joseph's dream of the sun, moon and stars and connect these two references...this is a reference to Israel and not Mary the mother of Jesus, nor to the church. Israel is depicted here as a woman who gives birth to a man child (Jesus, the Messiah). This man-child (Jesus) is caught up to God and to His throne (Revelation 12:5). Jesus is ascending to His throne in Heaven. This is referring to Jesus who is God the Son, ascending to His rightful place after He accomplished salvation. That rightful place is the throne of God because Jesus is God.

Now let's take a look at something wonderful in Revelation 14:12-13. We see that "someone" is saying: "here are they that keep the commandments of God and the faith of Jesus...and blessed are the dead that die in the Lord." At the end of verse 13 we see who it is that says these things. It is the Spirit, the Holy Spirit. He is speaking as a person, not an essence, and not only as a person but as God. So we have a wonderful appearance in these verses of Father, Son and Holy Spirit. They are always together. They are three in one...God.

Holy, Holy, Holy is the Lord God Almighty

Now it is very interesting here in Revelation 15 that we see a name used for God that is only found in Revelation. It is used in chapters before this one and after. I am going to suggest something that I will do no more than suggest because I can't prove it but want to present it to the reader. The name here for Jehovah God is "Lord God Almighty".

I am certain that this is a reference to God as one God yet in three persons. He is Lord and He is God and He is Almighty. In the same way, we see worshipers crying out to God saying "Holy, Holy, Holy is the Lord God Almighty" in Revelation 4. There are three holys and three names all referring to one God.

In Revelation 19:13 we see that Jesus is called by a new name and that new name is "The Word of God". This is just another confirmation that Jesus Christ is the Word of God just like John told us in the gospel of John. He is the Word, and this Word is none other than the one who created all things that were made and nothing exists apart from His creation. The Word of God is Jesus Christ who is God Himself.

In Revelation 21:5 we see that He who sits on the throne in Heaven says that He makes all things new. Then He continues on saying that He is Alpha and Omega; He is the beginning and the end and He gives freely to him that thirsts from the fountain of the water of life. The same speaker says He will give these who overcome an inheritance. He says He will be their God. We know as truth that Jesus says He is the Alpha and the Omega. He is the one who is, who was and who is to come (Revelation 1). We see in previous chapters in Revelation that it is Jehovah God who says He is the one who is, who was and who is to come, The Almighty. We can also look back to the story of the woman at the well. Jesus told her that if she would drink from the water He offered she would never thirst again; the living water. We know that Jesus is the living water and now in Revelation 21 it is the one who sits on the throne in Heaven calling Himself God who says He is all these things.

Chapter 22 brings us to the conclusion of God's Word and to the conclusion of all time. We see that there is one throne in Heaven and God sits on it but it is called the throne of God and the Lamb. John is overcome by this revelation of Christ and falls down at the feet of the messenger angel.

The angel tells John not to do it because he is just an angel, a servant like all of God's servants. Then he instructs John to worship God. It is clear that only God is to be worshiped, none other ever is worthy of His worship. Yet we know that all through the entire Word of God that Christ Jesus, pre and post incarnate, is rightly worshiped and always receives the worship given Him.

Jesus concludes by telling John again that He is Alpha and Omega, the beginning and the end, the first and the last. He tells John that He has sent **His** angel (only God can claim possession of His angels) to testify of these things.

At last the Spirit invites all who will come to Him to come and drink freely of the water of life which is God. The Spirit then gives final admonitions and promised blessings to the faithful in Christ. Then in Revelation 22:20 we hear the last Words of Christ in the Bible; and the Words are spoken by the Spirit who said just a few sentences earlier that it is Him, the Spirit, who is testifying of these things. Verse 20 says: "He which testifies these things says, 'Surely, I come quickly.'" We know it is Jesus who is saying that He is coming quickly yet the Spirit says He is the one testifying of these things. They are one.

Praise You Almighty God for Your precious truth. May You, by Your Spirit, open the hearts and minds of those who will read this. Help them to see these truths and trust in You today as God. Bless Your name Father, and come quickly, Amen!

Come to Christ Today and Be Numbered Among the Redeemed

Jesus Christ is Jehovah God. I believe that every single heart that has been made longs to believe this. I believe that even Jehovah's Witnesses long deep in their hearts to say and believe that Jesus Christ is God; because this is truth. My prayer to you reader, if you are one who denies the Deity of Christ, is that you will believe today and follow Him. He is waiting for you. Won't you enter His courts with thanksgiving and praise and gaze upon the unspeakable beauty of the Lord?

May the Lord bless you with the indwelling presence of His Holy Spirit, and may you become today one of the precious flock of God and be numbered among the redeemed...those who have been forgiven and cleansed from all sin. Christ died for you and is offering life, eternal life, to those who will be washed in the blood of the Lamb. It is only by grace through faith in Him and who He said He is that can save you and me. I am already among the redeemed of God and therefore have a place in Heaven with Almighty God forever. Nothing can change that. Won't you join me and all the others who have called upon the name of Jesus and have lived? I pray that you will.

Breinigsville, PA USA
30 December 2010
252459BV00001B/2/P